OPEN MIC NIGHT

OPEN MIC NIGHT

Campus Programs That Champion College Student Voice and Engagement

Edited by Toby S. Jenkins, Crystal Leigh Endsley,

Marla L. Jaksch, and Anthony R. Keith Jr.

With Robb Ryan Q. Thibault

Foreword by Wilson K. Okello

and Stephen John Quaye

STERLING, VIRGINIA

Sty/us

COPYRIGHT © 2017 BY
STYLUS PUBLISHING, LLC.

Published by Stylus Publishing, LLC.
22883 Quicksilver Drive
Sterling, Virginia 20166-2102

Library of Congress Cataloging-in-Publication Data

The CIP data for this title has been applied for.

13-digit ISBN: 978-1-62036-512-0 (cloth)
13-digit ISBN: 978-1-62036-513-7 (paperback)
13-digit ISBN: 978-1-62036-514-4 (library networkable e-edition)
13-digit ISBN: 978-1-62036-515-1 (consumer e-edition)

Printed in the United States of America

All first editions printed on acid-free paper
that meets the American National Standards Institute
Z39-48 Standard.

Bulk Purchases

Quantity discounts are available for use in workshops and for
staff development.
Call 1-800-232-0223

First Edition, 2017

10   9   8   7   6   5   4   3   2   1

This book is dedicated to youth spoken word artists.
You give us life.

Contents

It is easier to believe the stories fed to us
to write it as our own/ rinse and repeat like the scrubbing of our skin/
our calligraphy/ so there could be no trace of deception/
our voice so that it was always our choice/
until there is no whisper of the accent akin to your origins/
You emerge from this prison with false promises in your mouth
and nothing there to heal you/
We know differently
Mama showed us how to be well—every bowl of soup tasted of
revolution—she made being whole irresistible—
Told about a destiny—of things in flight—
this journey *ain't* of the feel good variety
not the rest your head don't cry baby/
this *ain't* for the light of heart, my child/ Are you sure, sweetheart?, that you
want to be well?. . . . Just so you're sure, sweetheart, and ready to be healed,
cause wholeness is no trifling matter. . . .

Okello (n.d.)

As members of society, we haven't been listening to the poets and artists whose resonances have traversed generations. For, if we were listening, the condition of our social and political ethics might not be in the fragile place that it is. Among the brave gone before us, Toni Cade Bambara (1980) raised a pointed question: "Are you sure you want to be well?" (p. 1). Wellness as dignity, subjectivity, and the liberties of personhood are not dispensed equitably in this world. If students are to achieve a wellness unscripted by rationality and the impulses of docility in which they are schooled, it will be brought about through a restructuring of the mind—a politics of indecency, audacious in spirit and authentic in approach. To loose the constraints of social realism that encumber our possibilities will require new modes of being. These imaginations will not fall from the sky; we will have to go and get them. As warrior poet Audre Lorde (1984) aptly reminds us in her poem "A Litany for Survival,"

our words will not be heard
nor welcomed
but when we are silent we are still afraid
So it is better to speak
remembering we were never meant to survive. (p. 255)[1]

(Re)member what it was like to fly, to go back and retrieve our red sea dreams, the allotment and longings we refused to surrender at the doorstep of our greatest fears. Poetics possesses that revolutionary potential, and *Open Mic Night* points the way forward, proposing that we listen with new ears to the possibilities for living that our students are sharing with us.

Clarifying for educators and witnesses alike, this text exemplifies and gives voice to the work of the "artivist." In his book, *It's Bigger Than Hip Hop: The Rise of the Post-Hip-Hop Generation*, M.K. Asante, Jr. (2008) defines the *artivist* as artist and activist, one who uses his or her talents to fight and struggle against injustice and oppression by any means necessary. The artivist merges commitment to freedom and justice with the pen, the lens, the brush, the voice, the body, and the imagination. The artivist knows that to make an observation is to have an obligation. Creating a rich archive of perspectives and stories, the contributors of this book allow students to be prophets of experience, rediscovering, confirming, and punctuating what they know to be true about the world. The voices in this volume take up, earnestly, the words of artivist Zora Neal Hurston (2017), who prophesied, "If you are silent about your pain, they will kill you and say you enjoyed it" (para. 3). The authors in this book refuse to go quietly. The questions for educators are, "Are we listening?" and "Are we willing to create the spaces for truth-telling and witness-bearing that will allow for wellness and new imagination?"

The editors and contributors of this book answer these questions for educators profoundly and weave poetry, spoken word, and personal storytelling to speak their truths loudly, boldly, and unapologetically. The rich tapestry that these authors weave with their words inspires hope, possibility, and change. They are stories of pain and struggle—the unending effort to foster spaces that enable them and others to live more fully in their bodies.

As the editors of this book convey, one of the consequences of schooling in the neoliberal paradigm in which we are currently nested is that it robs students of their intuitive sensibilities to become more than the "things" of social reproduction. This book resuscitates the most fundamental component of any move toward dignity and consciousness—desire. When desire is revived, the silenced, the oppressed, the dehumanized ask to be considered, refusing to be sealed into conformity or deference; recognition is demanded. Through the testimony of spoken word, poets become arbiters, creating new worlds and alternative ways of being that give shape to those desires. This is what the power voice looks like in this text.

We applaud the contributors for speaking truth to power, for refusing to merely be schooled and, instead, using their art to transform education. In the process, what readers see are bold voices that showcase the creative potential of art in its rawest forms.

Wilson K. Okello
Doctoral Candidate
Miami University
Oxford, Ohio

Stephen John Quaye
Associate Professor
Miami University
Oxford, Ohio
President, ACPA

Note

1. This extract is from "A Litany for Survival", from THE BLACK UNICORN by Audre Lorde. Copyright © 1978 by Audre Lorde. Used by permission of W. W. Norton & Company, Inc.

References

Asante, M. K. (2008). *It's bigger than hip hop: The rise of the post-hip-hop generation.* New York, NY: St. Martin's Press.

Bambara, T. C. (1980). *The salt eaters.* New York, NY: Random House.

Hurston, Z. N. (2017). Zora Neal Hurston quotes. Retrieved from https://www.thoughtco.com/zora-neale-hurston-quotes-3530194

Lorde, A. (1978). *The black unicorn: Poems.* New York, NY: WW Norton & Company.

Okello, W. K. (2017). *Of things in flight.* Unpublished manuscript. Oxford, OH: Author.

Identity is such a critical component of being both an artist and an arts administrator. Who are you? Why do you love art? How does it speak to you? What does it mean in your life? Through either creating or convening art, many of us engage in the process of continually discovering ourselves. So, as authors, it is important for us to share a bit of who we are and what we love so that you might understand why this topic is so dear to us. We are all former university administrators. Each of us has spent time working in student engagement, multicultural affairs departments, or both at four-year public universities. But we are more than that. We are all educators. We all currently serve in an educational capacity, either as a college professor or community-based educator. We love dynamic, creative, and engaged learning. But we are more than educators. We are all artists. Marla L. Jaksch is a formally trained artist, having attended the University of the Arts in Philadelphia. Crystal Leigh Endsley and Anthony R. Keith Jr. are internationally recognized spoken word artists. Toby S. Jenkins also writes and performs poetry as a personal hobby and a form of contemplative practice. And still, we are more than artists.

We are each daughters and sons of culturally rich and loving families and culturally complex communities, who share in a life experience of struggle, determination, resilience, and resourcefulness. It is important to understand all of who we are because these things have all influenced the campus arts events and programs that we have planned. This complicated experience makes us take everything seriously. A campus event space can't be wasted as simple entertainment. Life has taught us that we have important work to do. And so do you.

We wrote this book to help student affairs professionals explore the use of spoken word as a tool for college student engagement, activism, and civic awareness. Often when we think of performance on a college campus, the theater or art department comes to mind. While the field of student affairs often champions the need for arts opportunities on college campuses, there is not a rich body of literature that intentionally wrestles with the impact of dynamic, student-centered, and justice-oriented arts programs on college student development.

College campuses across the United States have been offering spoken word programs for more than 20 years, yet not much has been done in the field of higher education to critically understand these programs beyond their contribution to the campus social aesthetic. Scholars in English, ethnic studies, women's studies, and cultural studies have begun to understand that performance poetry and spoken word are much more than simple entertainment. Within these disciplines, scholarship has begun to surface exploring spoken word's role in developing political agency among young adults, its utility as a venue for authentic youth voice, and its importance as a tool of cultural engagement (Michalko, 2012; Wells & DeLeon, 2015; Youthspeaks .com, 2015; Chepp, 2014).

From our personal experiences in creating spoken word programs on college campuses and conducting research on cultural engagement as well as spoken word within educational settings, we have found that open mic nights make significant contributions to campus life. Open mic nights

- build community;
- create a space for student expression;
- offer a creative venue to channel students' social outrage and anger; and
- offer college students a way to speak out, advocate, lead, educate, and explore with their peers.

These programs often organically create an environment that encourages simultaneous expressions of vulnerability, humor, anger, and apathy—a space where students are allowed to be different.

These are critical spaces of personal development, intellectual development, and civic engagement. Student affairs practitioners must also begin to understand the educational and civic utility of such programs, which do so much more than simply open up a microphone for a college student audience. Spoken word programs allow college students to light the mic on fire by baring their souls.

This type of commitment to telling the authentic story and voicing the unique viewpoints of underrepresented communities forms the foundation of critical race theory. Hip-hop and spoken word artists probably wouldn't label themselves as theorists, but they are. Barnes (1990) offers an important explanation of the relevance of critical race theory in our work to serve and educate traditionally marginalized communities:

Minority perspectives make explicit the need for fundamental change in the ways we think and construct knowledge. . . . Exposing how minority cultural viewpoints differ from white cultural viewpoints requires a delineation of the complex set of social interactions through which minority consciousness has developed. Distinguishing the consciousness of racial minorities requires acknowledgment of the feelings and intangible modes of perception unique to those who have historically been socially, structurally, and intellectually marginalized in the United States. (p. 1864)

A critical component of acknowledging such feelings and modes of perception includes hearing the authentic stories of the cultural experience. As Delgado (1990) argues, people of color may speak from a very different experience. Thus, the concepts of authentic voice, story exchange, and naming one's own reality are essential to the critical race theorist (Delgado, 1990). These concepts are also critical to the hip-hop and spoken word artist, because hip-hop culture is largely about storytelling.

According to Banks-Wallace (2002), storytelling is a vehicle of preserving culture and passing it on to future generations. In some cases, stories can serve as touchstones that evoke shared memories and feelings between the storyteller and the listener (Banks-Wallace, 2002). As a touchstone experience, listening to another person's story may bring forth memories or feelings and can help the listener to better contextualize and understand her own experience—what it is to be a Black woman, what being a Latino male in the United States involves, or how poverty affects us all.

The technique of storytelling transcends race, class, generations, and other differences and allows people to communicate on common ground through a common story. Storytelling is universal. It has its roots in ancient African societies, and for centuries, people have used stories to entertain and educate as well as to instill values and inspire people to action. Describing storytelling as a new nontraditional approach to advocacy sounds strange, given its historical roots, but in modern times, with the advent of complicated electronic media communication methods, storytelling has become a lost art. Organizers and advocates often overlook the power of the spoken word and of shared experiences as a way of communicating and moving people to action. (Smiley, 2006, p. 74)

This is why we chose to include self-authored student essays and poems in this text. While the authors can synthesize existing literature and the primary data collected from our own research studies on culture, spoken word, and college student development, only students can tell the story of how spoken word has changed their lives, helping them to adjust, matriculate, and develop a sense of belonging on campus.

This book presents a mix of critical essays and college student writing (either current or former students) that explores spoken word, student engagement, and campus inclusion. Specifically, the essays share relevant scholarship on

- spoken word as an educational, civic engagement, and personal development tool (particularly among traditionally marginalized communities);
- the links between spoken word and social activism (art as social action, art as a form of civic leadership);
- the importance of privileging student voice in student affairs programming (even when they yell, even when they're angry);
- the challenges that come with engaging students in exploring intersecting concepts like race, gender, and class;
- considerations for creative and intentional spoken word programming (e.g., what does a creative program look like?); and
- scaling up for sustainability (through student affairs and academic affairs partnerships, study abroad collaborations, etc.).

Our hope is that this work helps to inspire, expand, and complicate the nature of the open mic night on college campuses. We have asked each of our student authors to share not only a reflective essay on the impact of spoken word in their lives but also a poem. Readers of this text need to interact not only with concepts and ideas but also with the art itself. We want you to take in the power of the words that young people write. And so, because this act of life authoring and reflecting through poetry is truly a request for vulnerability and openness, we have chosen to begin this book with our own poetry.

As educators and artists, we also must understand our position as a part of the very communities that we hope to create on campus. If our current or former students have been brave enough to publish their own art for the world to read, critique, and interpret, so should we. We hope that our poems can help you better understand the power of spoken word across generations and positions within education (young and old, student and teacher). By witnessing our attempts to artistically speak truth to power, we hope practitioners might be motivated to move beyond simply planning a program and strive to create critical spaces of growth, honesty, and communion that can speak to all of our souls.

Toby S. Jenkins, on why she wrote the poem "Love on My Sleeve":

> This poem was written to share at a campus open mic for a national day that is focused on depression called, "To Write Love on Her Arms." On this day, people around the globe are asked to write the word *love* on their arms and take pictures, post on social media, or showcase their body art as they go about their day. I answered the call both by writing the word *love* on my arm and writing a poem dedicated to anyone (but especially the young adults with whom I work) who might be suffering from the crippling grasp of depression.

Love on My Sleeve
I'm just trying to be . . . the kind of woman who wears LOVE on her sleeve
Takes her heart out willingly
Gives it some air . . . lets it breathe
Opens it up and allows it to be
The kind of design that can leave
Visual impressions on souls that bleed
I want to stitch my heart on leather jackets that keep souls warm on long winter rides
You know that kind of life that kinda feels like
You're climbing mountains and crossing rivers but will never get to the other side
And it's cold
And the bike is wobbling
And you feel unsteady
You're on this journey and no one even taught you how to ride
You are barely . . . hanging . . . on
And all you have to keep you going is the comfort of something warm
So let me be that material that can take a brick chill and turn it into something cozy
I'm ready to deal with hard and complicated
Ready to be a love that's not easy
That's not simple
I'm ready to be pricked by the needle, to pick up the thimble
And be the thread that stitches patterns of your life into a coat-of-armor
To cover you . . .
to help you keep riding until a new day breaks
I want to create
a brand name for that love called the Dawn of Carin'

For those like me
who still hope and believe
in the power of love and are refreshingly naïve
Enough to wear it on our sleeves

All I want to be is the type of woman who
carves love into the thick of her skin
Who recognizes emptiness, can empathize with loneliness,
Even if these are places I've never been
I can still reminisce with spirits that have strolled down paths
of persecution and judgment
Knocked on the door of dangerous liaisons
And cozied on the couch with the devil's advocate himself
I can walk with you because I've also made mistakes
And I'm that kind of brave heart that can take
an army of tattered, bruised and worn bodies and turn them into soldiers
I can turn inevitable defeat into the type of victory from which legends are
made
So take
My hand
And let's begin again
Your renewal was written . . . You see I etched it on my skin
I'm now wearing love as a tattoo
And that lasts longer than a safety pin or some super glue
My love for you
Isn't tacked on it is . . . carved . . . in . . . stone
My body is the rock
So just lean
And once you're rested
Once you've buried and invested
your burdens within my cracks and seams
Then you can start carving
a new vision of life, darling
And go ahead—show out
Make it a couture runway garment
But just be sure to create and leave
a little spot . . .
For a shiny red heart
That you can wear right there on your sleeve

Crystal Leigh Endsley, on why she wrote the poem "I Represent":

> This poem has been written and rewritten over several years. I begin
> many of my classes and workshops asking students to dig into the
> events, memories, and identities that make them who they are. It's only
> fair that I do the same. Each time I begin with this prompt, I have to
> revise this piece because my perspective on my own experiences has
> shifted. I was mostly trying to sum up all of the places and times that
> raised me, that shape how I make my decisions and where I find myself
> in life. I rarely perform any version of this poem at gigs. It felt safer to
> write it here.

I Represent
I come from a chipped set of glass bowls
Yard sales, and common sense.

I come from military housing projects
Summers of beach sunsets
Thick roots church roofs
Mixed girl complex
Tagging walls with beautiful text a stunningly designed mess.

I come from levee busting bayous
No church for the Beasts of the Southern Wild
Dancehall reggae styles Saturday night but Sunday
Morning finds a pew, hands raised.

I come from red dirt
Roads fried chicken livers and
Deer sausage greens from the garden
Tomatoes with skin so tight.

I come from sand grains
Choking on salt water
Undertow like ankle weights.

I come from tambourine praise
Praying until we sweat
Worship services singing stomping and keeping
Time hoping we go out to eat because we only
Ever do that on Sunday.

I come from distance
Misfit, black leather boots
Mama mad, daddy on a boat
Me and my brother in a silent truce
Signed with our eyes.
I represent the confusion, the uncertainty, the strong feeling but no clear map
The quick temper, lightning flash
The enduring questions that mark a parent's past
I represent that.

I come from white Nike ankle socks
Four times too big for me
Hand me downs but he wouldn't
Cold glares, icy hearts
But an apartment of warm feet.

I represent the patience it takes for a good roux to be made
Good things come to those who wait, my home school was the backyard or
the kitchen
Catching more than recipes if you were smart enough to listen,
Men and women, who demonstrate cooking is the oldest version of political
science,
I want to show you I love you so I fix you jambalaya

I represent the pregnant girl that goes to the emergency room to give birth
on the spot because insurance was not provided by her husband's job and
immigration might have laws, but love does not

I represent those who feel like their anger is all they've got

I represent every student that ever felt like they were wasting their time

I represent those that get accused of being afraid of commitment
it's just that mama raised me to be independent so pardon if I'm insistent
when it comes to putting my two cents in
literally

I represent the nerd who gets bullied at school who does the right thing even
when nobody else really cares

I come from silence stapled shut
Over my eyes. Invisibility is where I come from.
Learning to read at the age of three, read a book, read a situation, better off
being quiet
class room suffocating me
Stage rearranging me
Notepad saving me
I come from stars.

I come from a place mute with doubt
Swirled with drive, expectation, promise
Be bold, or you will be swallowed alive.
Stand up, or you will be forgotten. This is my greatest fear.
The daughter of a lion is a lion also.
I come from stars

Marla L. Jaksch, on why she wrote "*Whisper* to a Scream":

> This poem is about the power of community in creating pathways to heal-
> ing and the ways that collective work can produce love of self. Through
> our collective work, we learn who we are and what we can be. It is also
> a thank-you poem to those who have been a part of my coming to voice
> and action.

Whisper to a Scream

what that little girl needs, I need too
the need to know
say no
that what happened, happened
that it's pain she's feeling
that it's pain she's in
she's not depressed
she's not delusional.

Shame
for living
for having feelings about it
about being abused

about trust being shattered
about feeling broken
about fleeing myself
about that little girl leaving me, leaving us

I searched for her
make a space for her
I run
many returns
doubling back
doubling down
I begin to run in place
make a space
the sweat drips
I feel my body change
I hear words so tender they bruise
rearrange

When will I stop looking back
and how far?
I forgot about the future
written on my arm
the scar

For those in the struggle
either by choice
or because you have no other choice
personal and collective
alone or together, you
for those whose names I don't know
for those I couldn't say thank you to
When I couldn't manage, managed
for me
loved me
struggled for me
with me

to those who hug and comfort people they don't know—
because they can, because they know
to those who expanded my definition of love
to include
me

to those who smash shit
for those who build bridges
the makers, seers, doers, pathmakers, healers
to those who say fuck you to fear

who know truth speaks in many tongues
who know hope can be a fist raised UP

Anthony R. Keith Jr., on why he wrote "Starving Artist":

> "Starving Artist" is a declaration of artistic authenticity and humility.
> I know several professional poets whose sole source of income comes from
> writing and performing, and I admire them. I am inspired by their bravery
> and their unwavering commitment to live fulfilling lives as spoken word
> artists. As a professional educator and a poet, I want to ensure that I am
> always teaching, writing, and performing in truth.

Starving Artist

I'm a poet afraid to publish
I fear having a book with my words
And a back cover with blurbs like
"National best seller"
"A must-read"
"An awesome account of an artists' words"
I think it's absurd
For some, to use their art only for profit
I'm not trying to justify the life of a starving artist
But if art really is your gift then starving at some point should be a part of it
There should be some pangs in the pit of your stomach when your notebooks
are empty
And, ain't no more ink left in your pen
When you aren't changing lives and your paper is thin
I've accepted that at some point my economic reality
May rely on my poetic balladry
And I'm not sure my shit is as good as I think it is
But I know I am no longer willing to sacrifice my soul just to write some
fallacies
I've been asked to write wedding poems and birthday poems and poems
about anniversaries
Poems that spice up other people's love lives
And sometimes I feel dirty

And used
And confused
About whether they actually heard me
I wish I could turn the volume down on my poems
and transform my performances into a conversation
where I just be Tony Keith,
the poet, educator, and a nerd
I wanna be known as that artsy fartsy intellect that believes that there is power in his words
And that I not only took responsibility for what I said, but took responsibility for those that heard
Whether or not I pissed them off or convinced them to change the world
Let them know that sometimes I got tired
And sometimes I got weary, but I kept on writing
Even when my vision was blurry
Even when folks told me I needed to sit still
They'd say, "Boy, grass never grows under your feet"
I'd say, "That's because I'm way too busy climbing uphill!"
I'd tell them I don't have time to rest until the rest of my poems are written
But I can't stop writing so none of my poems have endings
Just transitions between new beginnings and space savers while refilling the ink in my pen again
Or moments when I need to stop, sleep, and dream just to recharge my system or
Moments when I need to set my pen on record and listen . . .
Listen—I'm trying to think myself through a literary breakthrough
Break down walls of bondage with poetic correspondence and make others feel uncomfortable
Make their stomachs feel unsettled while I keep pushing on these pedals 'cause I got no choice but to keep moving through
Because I'm doing what I'm called to do
And if you're open to receiving then the next call might be for you
And if you don't answer, don't worry
I'll be the collection agency when your payment is due
Granted, I've got a couple of degrees
And my account won't go completely in the red if I spend a few pennies
But I've got two cents to my name
And the life that I'm trying to live actually requires change
But I got bills
So I guess I'll keep paying with these poems
Hoping my soul will get filled

Some say, faith is what will get me through
Well if that's the case I invoke faith as my muse!
My power of attorney!
I want faith to take over when I can no longer take care of my self!
I want faith to take over when my ego can no longer control my wealth!
I want faith to be brave enough to pull the plug on my microphone
and wipe all my notebooks off the shelf!
Faith, don't be afraid to let me flat line!
Let me lay there until my heart gets back to beating at humble grind!
Resuscitate the power of God in my lungs
and let me breathe new poems . . .
Pure and simple ones
Poems about failure and poems about victory
Poems that rhyme occasionally
Poems that resist artistic prisons
Poems that break the chains of writer's block
And poems that enforce a pen can be a lethal system
I'm a poet afraid to publish
So I guess I'll have to keep publishing on these stages
And earn some kind of living on free open mic wages

References

Banks-Wallace, J. (2002). Talk that talk: Storytelling and analysis rooted in African American oral tradition. *Qualitative Health Research, 12*(3), 410–426.

Barnes, R. D. (1990). Race consciousness: The thematic content of racial distinctiveness in critical race scholarship. *Harvard Law Review, 103*(8), 1864–1871.

Chepp, Valerie. (2014). Speaking truth to power: Spoken word poetry as political engagement among young adults in the millennial age. Retrieved from http://hdl.handle.net/1903/15323

Delgado, R. (1990). When a story is just a story: Does voice really matter? *Virginia Law Review, 76*(1), 95–111.

Michalko, K. (2012). *The effect of spoken word poetry on the development of voice in writing.* Education Masters Paper 209. Rochester, NY: St. John Fisher College.

Smiley, T. (2006). *The covenant in action.* Carlsbad, CA: Smiley Books.

Wells, C., & DeLeon, D. (2015). Slam and the citizen orator: Teaching ancient rhetoric and civic engagement through spoken word. *Communication Teacher, 29*(4), 1–5. doi: 10.1080/17404622.2015.1058405

Youthspeaks. (2015). Brave new voices. Retrieved from http://youthspeaks.org/#

ACKNOWLEDGMENTS

Toby

This book is dedicated to all of the students who have crowded so many of my campus programs throughout the years. You came, you showed up, you showed out. We worked together to transform a campus into a community. We spoke our cultural experience into the halls of buildings that were originally created not to teach us. Thank you for your yells, shouts, tears, and silliness. College students keep you young, current, and laughing. Thank you for making my job feel like two decades of good times, joy, and love! To my partner, William, thank you for joining right into my family's cheerleading squad. You are always right there with my mom and dad, bragging, boasting, and being proud. That's what families do. To my mom and my Grandpa Joe, thank you for giving me poetry as a cultural legacy. And to my little Kai, thanks for dancing; singing; and reminding me that music, poetry, and hip-hop are the purest forms of joy.

Crystal

Many thanks to the Office for the Advancement of Research at John Jay College for its financial support as I pursued this project. Deep gratitude goes to Terri Moise and Caty Taborda-Whitt for sharing your stories first with me and now with the world. The work you have both implemented through the Feminists of Color Collective on Hamilton College's campus has changed lives. May the fires you have sparked continue to keep you warm. To JR, Nanyamka Fleming, Tracey Ogagba, Jessica Moulite, Anthony Jackson, Kevind Alexander, Andre, Adrian Marcano—to all my SpeakEasy family, I love you! To the faculty and practitioners who literally put their money where their mouth is and financially support the open mics we've written about here—thank you. In the context of my chapters here, I want to especially lift up Angel Nieves, Noelle Niznik, Nigel Westmaas, Amit Taneja, and Chaplain Jeff McArn. Thank you for showing up for me when it counted. To Toby Jenkins, Marla Lou, Tony my Starfish—I thank God for you. You three mean so much to me. Bats, I love you. Thank you for understanding that I have been called to give myself away. God, thank you for your grace. For the word. For the mic. For the people.

Marla

I would like to thank my students who challenge, inspire, and give me the opportunity to teach and learn alongside them. I also want to acknowledge great intellectual and creative debts owed to the many feminist artists and thinkers—especially hip-hop feminists—whose labor informs and gives rise to my contributions in this book. I want to say "Thank you" to my amazing collaborators and to Carla, Aman, and Sean, who make my creative and intellectual work possible by loving, caring, and nourishing the kids and me. Lastly, I want to thank my lovely Msabillah and Wangui. Mama loves you so much!

Anthony

To every student whose voice remains unheard and whose stories remain untold, I acknowledge you. To my partner, Harry, and my loving family, thank you for never allowing grass to grow under my feet . . . although I know you secretly wish I was still. And to Toby, Crystal, and Marla, let us continue to teach, write, and perform in truth, justice, and love.

INTRODUCTION

Robb Ryan Q. Thibault

Director of Student Life and Leadership/Hunt College Union at SUNY Oneonta

The slam can create . . . a family of many kinds of people who have learned to accept their differences . . . and still be a part of the family. . . . It challenges people to examine themselves, to take chances, to get to know people and ideas they would have otherwise just passed by. Each slam evolves in its own personal way, and that's a very important characteristic of what the slam movement is—celebrating differences.

Marc Smith (2003, p. 120)

Many of the contributors in this book have been impacted and transformed by the power of spoken word. My first poetry slam experience occurred in 1995 in the basement of the Cantab Lounge in Cambridge, Massachusetts. I walked into the venue unaware of what a poetry slam involved. However, shortly after my arrival, I was mesmerized by the diversity of people sitting together who ordinarily may not have shared the same space. They were sharing intimate stories and expressions of profound life experiences. These citizens were sharing their truths in a venue that fostered an openness of which I had never been a part. They were at times in vulnerable positions, being scored or judged for the glory of a small cash prize and bragging rights until the next week. For many people in this space, Sunday Mass was being replaced by Wednesday night slams. I witnessed a pivotal multicultural and community-building program, and this experience would linger deep into my professional career in college unions and student activities.

The slam was created in the mid-1980s in Chicago by the poet Marc Kelly Smith. Smith felt disconnected from the traditional poetry readings hosted in art galleries and university campuses, where it appeared only *learned persons* could appreciate the secret code of real poetry. Instead, Smith established poetry events in nightclubs (notably the Green Mill), events that were part jazz, part standup, and confessional in style. The slam debuted on a lark one evening as Smith simply added five judges from the audience to score poems on a 10-point scale. This created a kind of sports atmosphere as the audience responded to the scoring of judges by booing or with screams of approval. When a local *Chicago Sun Times* reporter asked Smith what he called these events, he responded that it was like a grand slam in baseball after a batter hits one into the stands and the fans go wild (Voedisch, 1986). Smith's intention was to use the slam as a mock competition or platform for the practice of effective writing and the art of performance. After all, a poet who can effectively use verse to engage and hold the attention of intoxicated patrons in a nightclub is impressive. In the early years, the poetry slam was often dismissed by academia as lacking artistic merit. However, as the slam grew and expanded globally in the late 1990s, its impact on the popularity of poetry both in popular culture (e.g., HBO's *Def Poetry Jam* and *Brave New Voices*, and the Tony Award–winning *Def Poetry Jam on Broadway*) and in the publishing houses was powerfully evident. The poets from these early days of slam who honed their skills in nightclubs and saloons have now gone on to complete MFAs and teach in colleges and universities.

In 1996 I took a position as assistant director for campus programs in the Memorial Union at North Dakota State University (NDSU) in Fargo. After six months I secured an off-campus venue to establish a poetry slam series at the First Avenue nightclub. Slam on the Plains became a popular Sunday night event for the Fargo-Moorhead area, connecting three colleges: NDSU, Minnesota State University–Moorhead, and Concordia College. True to form, this event attracted a wide array of people from across the area. I knew I was on to something. We worked hard to create a space where everyone's voice was welcomed. In April 1998 I worked with the NDSU union board to plan a special campus Grand Slam event for National Poetry Month. This event ultimately developed into the university's first live web-streamed event, whose execution brought together a collaboration of more than 20 campus officials in the early days of web services, networking, facilities, and the program board. The network data showed that we had listeners tuning in across the Dakotas, Minnesota, New Jersey, and even a listener in Norway.

As I developed my understanding of the college union field and its history, it became clear to me that the poetry slam is a contemporary link to the origins of the college union. College unions were born often as facilities to house debate societies. Spoken word, whether displayed in the intellectual grappling of ideas via debate or through competitive performed stanzas in the varsity sport of the soul, is central to our oral tradition and what it means to be human.

In November 1999 I was hired at the University of Michigan as a program coordinator in the Michigan Union. I was fortunate to establish the U-club Poetry Slam in fall 2000. It almost didn't happen. When I first proposed the idea during the spring budget season, I was met with a great deal of skepticism by a supervisor who quipped, "Michigan students wouldn't be interested in that." After the first two events drew several hundred students we pressed on. By mid-semester, we had the momentum to explore planning a collegiate poetry slam tournament in the spring. We worked with the local Ann Arbor Poetry Slam and the Association of College Unions International (ACUI) to coordinate the first national collegiate tournament in April 2001. It was a two-day tournament that drew six teams from seven colleges (University of Michigan, University of California–Berkeley, Eastern Michigan University, Yale University, Case Western Reserve, and Louisiana State University/Southern University). Sixteen years later, the College Unions Poetry Slam Invitational (CUPSI) has developed as a premiere ACUI student program, and in April 2016, 67 teams from across the United States, Canada, and for the first time a team from Europe (University of Edinburgh) participated in a four-day festival featuring open mics, workshops, and competitions to foster artistic and personal development and build community.

As one of the chief architects for the program and a student affairs practitioner, I am fortunate to have shaped, monitored, and assessed the growth and trends of the program over the years through tournament evaluation of every annual CUPSI event, as well as a series of ACUI poetry slam surveys codeveloped with Brian Magee at the University of Rochester and conducted between 2012 and 2015 based on 270 respondents across North America (Thibault and Magee, 2016).

Students involved in poetry slams are diverse across many identities and demographics. A poet profile of students in the survey reveals 57% identify as female, 7% as transgendered or gender nonconforming, 49% as LGBTQ, and 32% as AALANA (African American, Latino American, and Native American) students. The following statistics are also of note:

- Eighty-five percent of students agree that poetry slam participation provided them the opportunity to feel connected to their college.
- Ninety-five percent of students agree that the poetry slam on their campus was a meaningful part of their experience at college.
- Eighty-four percent of students agree that their campus poetry slam is a source for community building.
- Ninety-four percent of students feel part of a community when participating in their campus poetry slam.
- Ninety-three percent of students feel respect for ethnic and cultural differences at their campus poetry slam.
- Ninety-four percent of students feel respect for gender differences at their campus poetry slam.
- Ninety-eight percent of students feel respect for differences in sexual orientation at their campus poetry slam.

The most frequently cited learning outcomes identified by ACUI between 2009 and 2015 for students participating in poetry slam programs were growing meaningful interpersonal relationships, social responsibility, leadership development, enhanced self-esteem, and appreciation for diversity.

Spoken word events on campus through open mics or poetry slams are significant because they offer a barometer check on what is happening in our students' worlds. Listening attentively to the truths and personal narratives of our students provides us a timely and deeper or more textured understanding of what our student communities are struggling with, what they are celebrating and passionate about, and what direction they think our campus or national communities are heading. I often remind my peers that they need not rely on what they read in journals or college newspapers for information on student trends. I invite them, instead, to attend a slam or spoken word event to hear what's going on in our students' circles. Spoken word events serve as a means of connecting students with others; a path for exploring and understanding identities; a venue for pressing for social justice; and, when needed, a personal catharsis to process emotional and intellectual baggage that can obstruct achievement and success.

In my 15 years as a college union director at SUNY Oneonta, I have learned that the poetry slam can serve as a high-impact diversity and inclusion program and a nexus for connecting our students to the campus. For many of my students, our campus poetry slam (The Big O' Poetry Slam) and the evolving community we have established have been central elements in their cocurricular world. Since I arrived to SUNY Oneonta in the fall of 2001, we have crafted and sustained a powerful series, resulting in sending teams to the annual CUPSI event every year to date. Having reviewed 16 years of CUPSI tournament evaluations, the most consistent theme students express is *how they were positively transformed or shaped by the experience*. In 2002, one of my students was apprehensive about attending the CUPSI tournament. She claimed she had nothing in common with students from those "big prestigious schools" (Dartmouth College, University of Michigan, University of California–Berkeley, etc.) and felt she did not belong. When she returned from the event she was overjoyed and realized that while there could be obstacles between students from different colleges and identities, there were more bridges than barriers. She said it was the most powerful weekend in her college life. The aspiration to build community and create an honest and open space among like-minded, soulful students can prevail.

Art in all forms explores the good and beautiful and often serves as a lightning rod for social change. The nature of the poetry slam is provocative. One result from the ACUI poetry slam survey indicated that 55% of students felt respect for differences of political views at our campus poetry slam. In this turbulent period related to the impact of language on our campuses—with problematic poems and trigger warnings—I am concerned how campuses will foster constructive atmospheres that can support the spirit that everyone's voice is welcomed. A question I raise, and I hope that colleges and our nation will engage, is, can freedom of expression truly coexist with inclusion as we pursue building community?

As leaders cultivating spoken word, open mic, or poetry slam programs, how do we ensure a safe space where all students can express themselves freely and that emphasizes an openness to expressions that could challenge their notions or sensibilities? How can we offer students spaces where they can understand and create mechanisms to permit critical learning? Most important, how should we work with "ouch" moments when students are perceived to have used insensitive or insulting language? In our contemporary society it seems critical that educators must facilitate learning that helps students to rediscover civility in order to resolve conflict. This undoubtedly involves us working to create opportunities to challenge students for the sake of learning and personal development and reaffirmation to celebrate and understand our differences.

References

Smith, M. (2003). About slam poetry. In M. Eleved (Ed.), *The spoken word revolution: Slam, hip hop and the poetry of a new generation* (pp. 116–120). Naperville, IL: Sourcebooks.

Thibault, R. R. Q., & Magee, B. (2016). *The slam: One funky gumbo of poetry, identity, and transformation.* Presentation at the Association of College Unions International 96th annual conference, New Orleans, LA, March 22, 2016.

Voedisch, L. (July 25, 1986). Poetry boosters slam snob image. *Chicago Sun-Times.* Retrieved from https://www.highbeam.com/doc/1P2-3777052.html

I

SOUL MATES

When the Academic Scholar Meets the Street Poet

Toby S. Jenkins

"One truism in life, my friend, when that jones comes down . . . it'll be a mutha."

Addis Wechsler Pictures & Witcher (1997)

One of the most important questions I ask my colleagues, staff members, and students is, "Why do you do this?" Whatever your work might be, why do you do it? Is this simply what fell in your lap, or is this who you are innately? Many years ago, as a graduate student working diligently to breathe new life into the university cultural center, I came to know with certainty that the work I was doing was not simply an interest, passion, or even purpose—it was my spirit personified through programming. The rich cultural history about which we educated the campus, was my own—my historical giants and my cultural experiences, memories, values, and art. When a classmate and I sat down in 1999 to conceive an open mic program called the Juke Joint on the University of Maryland's campus, I pulled all of who I was into this program. The concept came from my childhood growing up in South Carolina, where juke joints were small, modest community spaces that came to life on Friday and Saturday nights. They offered those who worked the hardest, were paid the least, and struggled on a daily basis an opportunity to simply laugh, talk, and have a good time. Release. We wanted to offer this same type of space for our ethnically diverse college students on our predominantly White college campus. They also needed a space of cultural gathering and release.

During those early years of the Juke Joint, we worked hard to make the space historically accurate so that we were also educating students on African American history. We created a window counter called Otis's Fish Shack, where students could get free finger foods during the event. Otis was the

7

name of the first director of the Nyumburu Cultural Center at the University of Maryland. We paid so much attention to detail because our history and culture mattered to us. But we decided to make the Juke Joint more than a space for music and dance. We wanted it to be a central space on campus for students to share their opinions, ideas, life stories, and experiences.

I was a 22-year-old graduate student—a budding African American Gen-X professional. Two things were central to my identity at the time. The first was hip-hop culture, which framed my entire coming of age. The second blended hip-hop with another deep love of mine: poetry. I grew up listening to my grandfather recite his poems on his porch in South Carolina. Poetry was serious business in my family. My family basically forced the kids to write poetry; writing was like gold in our home. And so, in 1997, when a film titled *Love Jones* came out, I was officially smitten.

Love Jones is a beautiful love story. But what made it so incredible for us Black Gen-Xers was that it told the story of a young, cool, professional couple who was living life fully—pursuing their passions, falling in love, and communing with friends. This was our story. And the movie was rooted in the art of spoken word. The characters all convened regularly at a spoken word lounge. Each character either loved art or performed it—poets, drummers, and dancers. Set in Chicago, this movie put a major spotlight on spoken word. Early in the film, the main character, Darius Lovehall, shares a poem that I am sure, to this day, every *Love Jones* fan can still recite: "Say, baby . . . can I be your slave? I've got to admit, girl, you're the shit, girl, . . . and I'm digging you like a grave" (Addis Wechsler Pictures & Witcher, 1997).

This poem still makes me smile. It pays homage to the creative and artistic soul of Black folks, such as the ways we can make something as simple as asking a woman out into a work of art. This movie, this art, this cultural way of being made me proud of my community, so when I decided to merge this contemporary spoken word social scene with the history of the juke joint, this was more than campus entertainment. It was an act of cultural uplift— and it was incredible.

Our goal was quite ambitious. We didn't want to simply engage students. We wanted them to fall in love. The learning outcome was all about love. The goal was for them to fall in love with the program, their culture, and their voices. We wanted them to feel cared for and appreciated. We hoped that this program would be one of their fondest memories of college. We wanted this new campus experience to have the characteristics of any new relationship: anticipation and excitement. As one of the characters in *Love Jones* expressed, "When that jones comes down, it'll be a mutha . . ." (Addis Wechsler Pictures & Witcher, 1997). We set out for our programs to make students fall that hard, for them to walk in and feel that they had found their educational soul mate—that moment when academic scholar meets street poet.

I share this because when your work for students is a labor of love, your goals are a bit more organic and soulful than whatever is trending nationally as a learning objective. We didn't just want students to know and appreciate histories like the Harlem Renaissance; we wanted to re-create a modern renaissance experience that placed them on the stage as thinkers, activists, and intellectuals. We sought to create a space of inspiration, advocacy, and action.

During my six-year tenure on that college campus, the Juke Joint was one of the most successful campus events I ever witnessed. Hundreds of students attended each month. The venue filled to capacity every time. This program changed our campus. At that time, ours was a campus so deficient in service to ethnically diverse students that the Black Student Union had called for a protest of the Black cultural center for its lack of service. When we came to the cultural center and created this program, it was the start of a new energy within the cultural center. Finally, a major campus diversity program was consistently successful. Academically, students of all majors were writing and speaking; students were organically creating a community of support and love; faculty and staff entered the space as peer poets. As an administrator I have always performed at my open mics, because if I am asking students to bare their souls, so must I. But I came to the stage not as a staff member but as a person. I talked about social issues, relationship issues, family, community, and more. This is what reciprocal learning should look like.

We had no idea that what we were building was taking form as a campus tradition. Juke Joint was still happening at the University of Maryland in 2016, 17 years after I started it. I watched a YouTube video of a recent Juke Joint on that campus, and, like a proud mama, I was moved to tears that students who never heard of me were dancing, clapping, snapping, and communing at a program that I birthed. What about spoken word has allowed it to successfully engage college students for so long? Why do college students love spoken word so much? The answer might have something to do with spoken word allowing them to be real and to heal. Our students live in a society, and they come from external communities. They care about what is happening in the world. They need spaces to think, reflect, and speak.

Make Love, Not War

College students do care about what is happening in the world, and much of what is happening in our country makes them angry. Too often, the college campus has been treated as a safe bubble where young people retreat from the rest of society to learn, grow, and develop. They go away to school and leave their communities. The gates of our campuses often create a physical barrier between the college and the local community. More and more students are breaking free of the safe haven of campus and screaming for action and acknowledgment of issues like gender and racial injustice in the larger community.

In his book *Hip-Hop Culture in College Students' Lives*, Emery Petchauer (2012) helps us to understand the cultural value of resistant spaces or the *underground*, as they are known in hip-hop. According to Petchauer (2012), the notion of the underground is a contemporary hip-hop concept that communicates ideas of nonconformity, self-creation, personal freedom, and alternative space. Within hip-hop culture, the underground is the space where folks keep it real. The power structures of large commercial institutions can't intercede and control the thoughts and work production of underground artists. Campus open mics often create this same sort of grassroots alternative space. There is a sense of true intellectual and personal freedom, and in many ways, the student audience actually creates and controls the environment. While practitioners might build the opportunity, guide the ground rules and expectations of the community, set the tone, and put together the event pieces that establish the open mic, the student audience naturally creates and determines what this program will become and what this space will be on campus. While we know the idea of the underground to be a construct— a part of a language that those within the culture of hip-hop immediately understand—the underground is not just philosophical. It involves "real places populated by real bodies" (Petchauer, 2012, p. 30). In his study of hip-hop culture on multiple college campuses, Petchauer (2012) enters the lives of several college students who are deeply involved in hip-hop in some form—emceeing, DJing, performing spoken word, dancing, painting graffiti, or being an active fan. He shares how the campus open mic helped one student to form identity:

> The Word Perfect open microphone event was responsible for his public development and identity formation as an emcee within the campus community. Two Thursdays each month . . . a transformation occurs in the west wing of the Colonial student center. By day this area is populated by students sitting at tables eating food from the adjacent cafeteria. At night, Headz Up converts the area into an underground space. Rows of chairs totaling 300 replace cafeteria tables on the carpeted floor. Students from groups such as Black Student Alliance and the Latino Student Alliance fill chairs and jump up and scream when the host of the evening shouts them out in a ritualistic roll call. Instead of looking down at cafeteria food or class notes to cram before a test, students gaze at the glowing stage up front

where fellow students or invited performers showcase everything from poems scribbled in class to songs labored over for months. Whether it's spoken word, hip-hop, soul, R&B, or comedy—Word Perfect is a chance to show and prove. (Petchauer, 2012, pp. 35–36)

Even the name of this event speaks volumes to its role in the lives of students. "Word Perfect" can mean a variety of things. It might mean the challenge to produce outstanding work. It communicates that the classroom is not the only educational space where students are striving for an A. But the title, "Word Perfect," also pushes us to understand the power of words—that words are perfect weapons for confronting injustice. In her foreword to the book *Talking Back and Looking Forward: An Educational Revolution in Poetry and Prose*, Antonia Darder (in Gorski, Sacledo, & Landsnab, 2016) asserts that language and creativity are important weapons for struggle and that educators must be committed to incorporate the "often negated cultural wisdom at work in the everyday lives of both students and teachers" (p. xiii). She goes on to state,

> Our labor for justice requires teachers to be willing to access, then, whatever skills and resources are available to us so that we may speak truth to power while we simultaneously create a place for the silenced histories of those never consulted to move to the center of the discourse. (Darder, in Gorski et al., 2016, xvii)

The use of a word like *weapon* conjures up images of war and conflict, concepts we associate with a military base rather than a college campus. But ours is a space preparing students to address the complicated issues and problems facing our society and our world. As a place of scholarship, we should be building student capacity to use whatever resources they possess—their minds to think critically, their words to educate and challenge, their bodies to protest, and their hands to create and build. Undoubtedly, our country is now experiencing another civil war of sorts. We are at odds regarding what justice should look like in the United States. When civil wars—in the form of riots driven by issues of race, culture, politics, and poverty—are fought by everyday people, those unaffected can easily forget the lasting devastation. Just as the daily realities of a foreign war often go unknown by many Americans living thousands of miles away from the war zone, we are also often unaware and oblivious to the continued challenges that our own citizens face as they seek to heal themselves physically and spiritually from internal political rage.

But to truly heal our nation, we must become more connected to the problems of others, more aware of the oppression that exists, and more willing to work to make a difference. Quite plainly, we need to hear and listen to one another, because when we come together to honestly talk, tell, yell, cry, or even scream, the humane core of our selves is moved to change. So rather than barricading students behind the safe walls of campus, we need to allow them to think, speak, and act as educated citizens.

Spoken word and the hip-hop culture that includes it are such spaces of critical engagement. Building on the work of Paulo Freire and Henry Giroux, Petchauer (2012) offers the field of critical pedagogy as an important theoretical basis for understanding the ways that spaces like open mics create learning environments that promote critical thinking:

> Critical pedagogy asks "how and why knowledge gets constructed the way it does, and how and why some constructions of reality are legimated [*sic*] and celebrated by the dominant culture while others are not." . . . From this perspective, critical consciousness refers to the ability to recognize that knowledge and metanarratives that communicate how "people are" and why "things happen" are not neutral. Rather they privilege some groups and disadvantage others. (p. 89)

Ultimately, educators who dare to create alternative or underground spaces, which are essentially spaces of freedom and liberation, are engaging in the very important act of loving students—loving their lives, their voices, and their ways of knowing. When we work diligently to create a central space within academia for the divergent voice, the critical voice, and the non-dominant perspective, we are simultaneously fighting injustice and engaging in the loving act of recovery. We are creating change.

In all moments of great intensity, disaster, and importance we are often humbled to the core of what it means to be human. As a result, we leap head-first into acts of love that are meant to change the social condition of our world. Examples of broad social events—such as the attacks of September 11, 2001; Hurricane Katrina; and the earthquake in Haiti—move people to a greater level of consciousness, a greater sense of what it is to be human, and a higher plane of leadership. Even moments of personal tragedy, such as a major disease diagnosis, or life-changing events, like a divorce, cause us to remember love and care for the spirit. Amazingly, the moments of struggle against racism, sexism, classism, and oppression in communities have the same effect. Like survivors of a storm, the oppressed often come together and share their storm stories and do the work of loving themselves back to life. These moments of struggle always bring us face-to-face with spirituality and love. How we choose to act is often an expression of how we choose to love.

Whether expressing rage, frustration, sadness, or desperation, ultimately we are reacting to lovelessness in our society. As bell hooks (2001) points out in her book *Salvation*, love's relationship to politics, leadership, and social struggle is a needed body of scholarship yet to be explored:

> Since our leaders and scholars agree that one measure of the crisis people are experiencing is lovelessness, it should be evident that we need a body of literature, both sociological and psychological work, addressing the issue of love, its relevance to political struggle, its meaning in our private lives. (p. 5)

Art has been this type of vehicle for expressing political critique and exhibiting authentic love for a society—the type of commitment that causes you to speak out when you see your society going in the wrong direction. We criticize out of love—out of a wish to make things as best as they can be. The art produced by historic and contemporary artists is a love story filled with all of the drama that comes with being crazy in love—intense feelings, differing perspectives, unintended neglect, and inexplicable attraction. Through song, paint, voice, camera, and computer, artists give life to issues that matter. Though stereotypically viewed as angry and radical, protest movements and writings and activist art are truly attempts to create a love-driven world. Moreover, the work that protest artists produce must begin to be examined as important acts of love and examples of authentic critical education.

After 10 years of working within student affairs administration in higher education, I know how easy it is for administrators to view student protestors as agitators—to see protest as a problem. It is a solution—a wake-up call. And I argue that those students who dare to protest are showing more school spirit and more commitment to citizenship than those who simply attend every football game, wear paraphernalia, and yell their love for their school or their country with all their might. In a broad sense, I am concerned that our country raises citizens who are not taught how to be critical thinkers—to question, to learn, to criticize the status quo. We often define *patriotism* through kind and pleasant words rather than strong and bold action. In a broad sense, we groom students to play a very docile, silent, and inactive role in school. Whether protesting the perils of our society or the problems on our campuses, student voices of dissent and criticism need to be heard. We must encourage students to engage college not simply for the sake of attaining a degree but more importantly to make a real contribution to our world. The following statement from William Barclay (2001) sums it up perfectly:

All human things are trivial if they exist for nothing beyond themselves. The real value of anything depends on its aim. If we eat simply for the sake of eating, we become gluttons, and it is likely to do us far more harm than good; if we eat to sustain life, to do our work better, to maintain the fitness of our body at its highest peak, food has a real significance. If people spend a great deal of time on sport simply for the sake of sport, they are at least to some extent wasting their time. But if they spend that time to keep their bodies fit and thereby to do their work for God and for others better, sport ceases to be trivial and becomes important. The things of the flesh gain their value from the spirit in which they are done. . . . The most important thing is the life-giving power of the spirit. (p. 265)

We can extend this to include the life-giving power of art. When art is used as a tool of social activism, it ceases to be mere entertainment. It becomes an important piece of knowledge production. Contemporary and street-based poetry is a vehicle of such activism and leadership, and it is a space for critical education and social engagement for college students.

When I reflect on myself as a young college student in 1997 watching *Love Jones* for the first time, I remember being excited to try my hand at writing my poetry to a rhythm that could be performed. I was excited by the possibility of writing poetry that was real talk and not high art. In writing this chapter, I remember not only my first program as an arts administrator but also my first experiences as a spoken word artist. Spoken word continues to be a major part of who I am and how I engage my work as an educator, but it first served as a critical space for me to wrestle with acquiring new knowledge about race, culture, and history. I recently edited the hip-hop section of a book in which Mazi Mutafa wrote a chapter on being a community-based hip-hop educator. In his chapter, Mutafa (2017) asserts that the educators who create hip-hop–based programs are really the adult versions of the kids who need these spaces. In my case, this was definitely true. I not only create these spaces but also work hard for them to be exceptional and sustainable, because the hip-hop and spoken word culture has also sustained me through life. The work is personal, meaningful, and important.

References

Addis Wechsler Pictures (Producer) & Witcher, T. (Director). (1997). *Love jones* [Motion Picture]. United States: New Line Cinema.

Barclay, W. (2001), *The gospel of John: The new daily study Bible*. Louisville, KY: Westminster John Knox Press.

Gorski, P., Salcedo, R., & Landsnab, J. (2016). *Talking back and looking forward: An educational revolution in poetry and prose.* Lanham, MD: Rowman & Littlefield.

Hooks, B. (2001). *Salvation: Black people and love.* New York, NY: Harper Perennial.

Mutafa, M. (2017). Community-based hip-hop education. In C. P. Gause, R. Majors, & T. Ransaw (Eds.), *The handbook of research on Black males* (pp. 54–73). East Lansing, MI: Michigan State University Press.

Petchauer, E. (2012). *Hip-hop culture in college students' lives: Elements, embodiment, and higher edutainment.* New York, NY: Routledge Press.

Student Voices

Jason Reynolds

Alumnus, University of Maryland

Poet Self-Portrait

I've heard it spoken about all kinds of ways, punch-lined in stand-up bits, caricatured in romantic movies. But, to me—for me—it isn't hyperbole to compare it to a kind of secular sanctuary, a church where all are priests and proselytes among themselves, taking turns in the pulpit, testifying, edifying, laying prostrate publicly at the feet of an intangible presence weighing heavy on the room. It was where people came to double down as double-talkers, came to test their limits as tightrope walkers, balancing the humility of uncertainty and the absolute arrogance of professing to know all. This was where 17 meant sage; where outspoken intellect, even when empty, was seen as sexy; where shoulders could roll back, and teeth could cut, and eyes could water, and voices could crack, and throats could strip, and the names and checked boxes that lit up computer screens in the offices of administration and bursar could disconnect from the empirical and exclaim that which was emotional. This was the open mic, which at the University of Maryland–College Park we called the Juke Joint.

I was 16 the first time I went, but the first time I went doesn't matter without acknowledgment of what led me there. I'd started writing poetry, seriously, in high school, completely unaware that people referred to its performative style as *spoken word*. To me, it was simply Langston Hughes, Nikki Giovanni, Lucile Clifton, Rita Dove, Gwendolyn Brooks, Sonia Sanches, Amiri Baraka, Haki Madhubuti, word word word, line break, word word word, line break, new stanza, new stanza, gut punch, short and swift to the reader, unassuming, unintimidated, lured, comforted by the mass of white space. Poetry was a way to feel better about hating to read and write, but loving to say the things I was thinking. Deft communication.

My mother was the one who told me to project. To recite my poems like they meant something. To speak them loud enough so as to not lose the people in the back, though the people she was referring to didn't exist yet. So that's what I did. I had not been particularly extroverted, nor did I possess a penchant for drama. I was just a mama's boy, and whatever she told me was the right way to do something, that's the way I tended to do it.

So I practiced projecting all through high school and got pretty good at it, too. Wound up in college at 16 with nothing but 2 less years on my life than everyone else, an anxious tremor in my belly, and poetry—poetry that I'd learned to project. So a month into my collegiate career, I signed up for the school's talent show, where I recited a poem, where I would nervously lift my voice in a way that wouldn't lose the people—now *actual* people—in the back. A projection of voice, and of the imminent, as that moment would go on to change my life.

At that event I'd meet the three people who would become my creative ushers. The first was Delonte. Delonte was a senior, a Black neo-bohemian, aptly (for the time) outfitted with locs, leather moccasins, and a nose ring. Delonte was the college kid who was way too cool for college. Never seemed to be working, and that seemed to be working for him. He always sort of floated above campus, a scent of patchouli and marijuana always trailing behind him. A confidence I had never seen. He was also plugged in to the Washington DC arts scene, and after connecting the night of the talent show, he started driving me—Delonte also had a car—off campus to U Street, which was the mecca of creative expression in the city at the time. It was Delonte who would haggle with doormen to get them to allow me, under-aged, entry into what seemed to be an underground circuit of aboveground coffee shops that doubled as open mics at night. To me, they were thunder rooms. They were prayer closets, magic spaces where I, at 16, could see into the future.

The second person I met that night was the exact opposite of Delonte. Instead of locs, he wore his hair in a permed, bright-red afro, and instead of moccasins, he preferred alligator boots. A White boy with an instinct for flair, who happened to share my name—Jason. Jason introduced himself to me the night of the talent show almost as though he was in the market for friends. I had been used to seeing him strolling around campus in tailored suits, and the way people spoke about him was as if he, too, floated above the rest of us. But after our first conversation, it was made clear that his image on campus was simply a force field, and that behind all the regalia was an irrever-ent fine artist. We became roommates the following year, had written a book together by the time we were seniors—my poetry, his art—and soon after moved to New York together, where we landed our first major book deal.

The third person I met the night of the talent show was Tony. He was different from the other two. He came offering just a simple handshake, a smile, and an opportunity to submit a poem to the campus's Black newspa-per. He was also a poet, and our love for language would forge a fast friend-ship. Tony also invited me to the Juke Joint.

I was 16 the first time I went.

I don't remember a list, or even a host, though there may have been one. All I remember is the feeling of finding a home on a sprawling campus of

40,000. I, 16 years old and suffering from severe imposter syndrome, now had a place to come once a month to bear witness to other imposters, others' insecurities. I could find mirrors in their guttural voices and their poems, and I could offer another slice of humanity—sometimes ugly, sometimes lovely—to this pot we all were stirring.

We didn't know what it would become. To us, our fellowship was just that, a fellowship. A place to share. But perhaps we were, unbeknownst to us, performing a kind of incantation, a beckoning to other students who were looking for an outlet.

By the time I was 17, the handful of us had become a hearty gathering. And by the time I graduated, there were hundreds of people jammed inside a small room in the campus's cultural center every month.

There were lists then. *Long* lists. And hosts. Shaky paper in hands. Cocky a cappella raps. Stammers and stutters. Screaming and crying. Laughter and sexuality. Me, as a senior, watching me, as a freshman, on stage at the talent show triangulated by soon-to-be lifelong friends—friends who clap, even if only for courage.

For teenagers who could be ambivalent, we were engaging, hearing, seeing, and saying the things we were thinking and feeling. For teenagers, many of whom, like me, had just been taking their mother's words as absolutes, who had been maybe *projecting* in other ways, the Juke Joint had become a space to bravely scrape the scabs from our kid skin.

And our poems, well, they were our fingernails, scraping scraping scraping.

Slick Talk

someone once told me i was born to be
mute born to be matte
polish is for the unscratched
they said and i got scratches
too many scratches
scrapes like canals in my veneer
they said scrapes like canals
would catch the polish
cause it to build up
make my surface be shine but bump
and don't nobody want nothing imperfect
they can see their own reflection in
they said

and i thought
they wrong
they wrong
because if I was born to be mute
made to be matte
shot out to shut up
then why
why
why would God
fashion me such a slick tongue?

2

THE SPOKEN WORD EXPERIENCE

Shifting Student Learning From the Classroom to the Stage

Anthony R. Keith Jr.

L earning is most evident when students are able to recognize and articulate their cultural narratives within an affirming educational space.
Schools, colleges, universities, and community-based organizations
need to have a modicum of understanding about the cultural experiences of
the students they serve in order to teach them effectively. Spoken word poetry
is an experience likely shared by many students who enter the higher education environment, especially students of color who come from urban communities. "Spoken word poetry is a form of poetry that utilizes the strengths
of our communities: oral tradition, call-and-response, home languages, storytelling and resistance" (Desai & Marsh, 2005, p. 71). Assigning value to
the cultural assets of a community within education is one of the aims of
critical pedagogy; thus, there is a need to broaden the connections between
students' cultural literacies and the conventional English curriculum (Bruce
& Davis, 2000). In addition, by ignoring students' valuable cultural assets,
education becomes a meaningless instructional process (Rodriguez-Valls,
2009). Spoken word poetry is, as a result, not only an entertaining form
of artistic expression but also a tool for student learning and engagement
within academic institutions and educational organizations. In this chapter,
I explore some of the theoretical and empirical underpinnings that influence
how students engage with spoken word poetry within educational environments. Specifically, I examine themes emerging from the literature that connect spoken word poetry to student critical literacy practices, teacher agency,

student efficacy and identity development, hip-hop pedagogy, and social justice.

Spoken Word Poetry as a Critical Literacy Practice

Within the broader context of culturally relevant pedagogy, Freire (1970) introduced the argument for implementing a curriculum that emphasizes the need for the oppressed to engage in a critical and affirming pedagogy constructed around student and teacher narratives. Ernest Morrell, professor of English education and director of the Institute for Urban and Minority Education at Columbia University, expands upon Freire's work through his research on critical literacy and urban youth. According to Morrell (2005), spoken word poetry is an art form that combines traditional notions of reading, writing, and speaking with bodily performance and is a part of urban students' cultural literacy practices. This perspective is further supported by Camangian (2008) and Bruce and Davis (2000), who argue that teachers must develop pedagogy that disrupts culturally reproductive consequences of school and classroom alienation for students considered "less educated." Furthermore, they suggest that poets can manipulate the standard forms of English and use the language with license in terms of structure, rule, and meaning.

Similarly, Biggs-El (2012) postulates that the absence of qualitative aspects of teaching and learning in the school curriculum leaves young people in the nation's inner cities to their own creative devices in terms of how they practice literacy and the art of expression. "Critical literacy encourages the deconstructing of power, values and attitudes in text and positions text as a form of empowerment for some social groups, all of which places it in direct opposition to the established traditions in English classrooms" (Lopez, 2011, p. 78). Those countertexts can be in the form of social action, performance poetry, dance, music, and other expressive forms, which refer to a way of understanding and engaging in culturally relevant pedagogy in English classrooms.

Therefore, spoken word poetry falls within the realm of critical pedagogy, because it defies normative schooling practices, and illustrates the reflexivity of the performing arts to subvert racial oppression and address social justice and equity (Biggs-El, 2012). According to Desai and Marsh (2005) utilizing spoken word poetry in the classroom engages students and teachers in a dialogue that draws from their lived realities and facilitates collective meaning making. Thus, using spoken word poetry as a strategy to shift the focus away from academic deficits of urban students and to the cultural assets those students bring with them to school every day is culturally relevant pedagogy

(Wissman, 2010). Furthermore, the kinds of poetry used in many U.S. urban classrooms rely heavily on the "classics," where the focus is primarily on the experiences of "dead white men" who are not culturally representative of the student demographic (Jocson, 2005, p. 133).

Historically, the development of spoken word poetry was born out of the Black Arts Movement (BAM) in the 1960s as a political and artistic response to racism in the United States. Fisher (2003) explores the connection between contemporary spoken word poetry and BAM as a critical approach to frame an ethnographic study of performance poetry venues (open mics) in predominantly African American communities. Named as African Diaspora Participatory Learning Communities (ADPLC), Fisher (2003) suggests that her participants are involved in multiple literacy practices through the spoken word, which deliberately draws on the need to sustain Black cultural literacy practices. The blending of oral and written traditions culturally relevant to African American communities forms these multiple literacies. Youth engagement with spoken word poetry (YSW) began in the United States around 1990 as a public discourse characterized as directly resistant to dominant models of communication and social interaction (Weinstein & West, 2012).

In their critical analysis of the YSW movement, Weinstein and West (2012) argue that researchers need to collaborate with poets, poet-teachers, and arts institutions in order to turn a critical eye on the field and maintain its integrity in the midst of growth and development. Furthermore, Williams (2015) theorized that youth involved in a volunteer youth spoken word poetry club at a local library demonstrated the varied possibilities for incorporating this medium within the English classroom. In particular, students could use poetry alongside their study of political and social history, employ figurative devices learned in their traditional English classes, and engage in self-expression and reflection. Last, findings from Smith's (2010) study indicate that the processes of creating and performing literature provide students opportunities to interrogate school-sanctioned intelligences and challenge beliefs about literacies and the purpose of literacy learning in the academy.

English Language Learners

Elting and Firkins (2006) present an argument that English language learners (ELLs) can explore the aesthetic function of language and develop confidence in using English as a communicative tool through the dramatization of poetry. Referred to as *verbal art*, Elting and Firkins (2006) conclude that ELLs' engagement with performance poetry develops their ability to infer meaning by interacting with text. In their experiences as ELL teachers, Elting and Firkins (2006) indicate that students make use of different body language, facial expressions, gestures, and creative voices to demonstrate English language acquisition. Hadaway, Vardell, and Young (2001) make a similar claim that poetry is a uniquely appropriate vehicle for providing space and pleasure in oral language skill development for ELLs. In their explanation of scaffolding oral language through poetry for students learning English, Hadaway and colleagues (2001) suggest that ELLs increase their language fluency through hearing and reciting poetry, which in turn builds their confidence with English communication.

Spoken Word Poetry as Teacher Agency

Some teachers have difficulty accepting spoken word poetry as a valid academic utility as well as experience challenges with learning how to incorporate poetry performance in their classrooms (Jocson, 2005; Reyes, 2006; Rodriguez-Valls, 2009; Watson, 2013). Findings from Fisher (2005) suggest that the racial and ethnic identity of teachers and teacher-poets could have an effect on the level of student engagement with spoken word poetry. For example, what happens when students' poetry embodies inner-city street vernacular (slang) and volatile subjects that offend teachers or that challenge traditional standards of writing and language? Conclusions from Watson's (2013) study indicated that teachers struggled to find students' narratives of poverty, anger, and injustice academically acceptable. However, denying students access to multiple literacy tools that help them effectively code-switch further stagnates academic achievement (Watson, 2013). What creative agency do teachers have in accepting cultural literacy practices of their students? What does this mean for state-mandated learning outcomes and performance assessments? For many teachers, it requires the involvement of teacher-poets from the community to provide cocurricular instruction and spoken word poetry programming in and out of school (Jocson, 2005; Stovall, 2006; A. Wiseman, 2010a, 2010b, 2011).

Jocson (2005) analyzed the implementation of the Poetry for the People program (P4P), a culturally inclusive poetry curriculum intervention developed by the late June Jordan—a Caribbean American poet, essayist, and activist—in an urban high school. Teachers in the Jocson (2005) study were required to collaborate with student-teacher poets (STPs) who provided weekly supplemental instruction on spoken word poetry using the P4P curriculum in their English classrooms. Some of the teachers expressed feeling a lack of agency in making decisions about pedagogy and curriculum. In contrast, some teachers saw the value in some of the curricular material and adopted it as their own for use in future poetry units.

What happens, however, when teachers have creative agency in their pedagogy and English curricula? Lopez's (2011) case study investigated one teacher's agency and activism in a secondary English classroom in Canada. The policy mandate for 12th-grade English in Ontario, Canada, provides English teachers the opportunity to implement alternative pedagogies and develop agency that disrupts the dominant and Eurocentric forms of knowledge and discourses prevalent in many schools. Lopez (2011) wanted to know in what ways critical literacy might open up spaces for student engagement in diverse English classrooms.

Incorporating elements from Camangian's work (2008), Lopez (2011) presented findings from a case study documenting an English teacher's approach to developing a curriculum that included a local spoken word artist as a cofacilitator for a unit on performance poetry. The teacher in Lopez's (2011) study created a conceptual model of critical inquiry for deconstructing performance poetry comprising five phases that help students construct their own performance poetry based on their own lived experiences: deconstruction, critique, collaboration, reflection, and action. The teachers evaluated students on their use of poetic literary devices such as imagery, voice, structure, and organization. All students passed the unit, demonstrated higher achievement scores, and increased their engagement and participation in class.

Reyes (2006) described his agency as an urban middle school English teacher as a need to understand how to navigate around the politics of education for his students that would enable them to liberate themselves from whatever limited them in their lives. Reyes further explained, "I quickly discovered that despite how these children love their poetic words, nowhere was there an opportunity to explore their identities as poets within the Language Arts content standards nor in the adoption of my district's scripted curriculum" (2006, p. 11). Reyes implemented a voluntary after-school spoken word poetry program for the students that focused on transforming the physical environment, hosting a spoken word poetry workshop, and building identity and the language of poetic discourse. He argues that giving student-poets opportunities to find themselves through the culture of poetry helps them take more control over growing into the person they want to become.

Situating spoken word poetry as a cultural literacy practice after school may serve as an additional site to examine teacher's agency. "Out-of-school settings are important context for this work because research has shown that these alternative knowledge spaces are where literacy learning is authentic and purposeful for multiple generations of color" (Fisher, 2003, p. 363). Findings from Wiseman (2010b) suggest that writing poetry encourages a collaborative learning model in the class and positions teachers as literary resources, and writing for performance and publication provides an authentic purpose for students. Last, Rodriguez-Valls (2009) utilized culturally relevant poems, suggested by students' families, in implementing an English arts curriculum that complemented the state's standardized education requirements.

Spoken Word Poetry as a Reflection of Student Identity

Turning an identity lens onto a specific adolescent literacy practice such as spoken word poetry is important for those who regularly engage with teenage students (Rudd, 2012). Desai and Marsh (2005) engaged 10 students in a voluntary after-school spoken word poetry course and found those students were arguably more willing to articulate how they feel about their social realities in that space than they were in their traditional classrooms because their identities and literacy skills were not trivialized; they were validated. Similarly, Rudd's (2012) ethnography examined how participation in a school-sanctioned poetry competition team (slam poetry group) affected the identities of the student team members and the group. Through an analysis of interviews with student poets and observations of the team's practice sessions and community performances, Rudd (2012) found that students' participation in slam poetry engaged them in a complex and fluid identity-formation activity. Desai and Marsh (2005) also suggest that spoken word poetry helps students realize that they are literate and able to engage in critical dialogue and action.

All members of Rudd's (2012) study identified themselves as "social outcasts"—or at least different from mainstream adolescents—and spoken word poetry served as a creative vehicle that validated their respective identities within and outside the group. Conversely, Bruce and Davis (2000) and McCormick (2003) discuss notions of social isolation as a byproduct of socioeconomic and political conditions. In a critical analysis of "at-risk" student identities in urban schools, McCormick (2003) presents an argument that poems can serve as illustrations of violence within the student's communities, thereby resulting in their performance of a violent identity in school, which predicates the school's disciplinary and safety policies.

A similar argument is presented in Bruce and Davis's (2000) appeal for educators to use spoken word poetry as a method to curb youth violence in public schools, promote empathy, and improve students' public speaking and literacy skills. Their findings suggest a connection exists between their students' engagement with spoken word poetry and their capacity to develop confidence, pride, emotional maturity, and understanding. Furthermore, findings from Rudd's (2012) study suggest that teachers need to be cognizant that nontraditional forms of literacy and a group membership tied to that literacy have the potential to positively impact adolescents' identity formation.

Camangian (2008) suggests that spoken word poetry serves as a powerful means of self-representation for youth traditionally portrayed as threatening and incapable of managing their temperaments. One of the stories shared in the Camangian (2008) article was about an English teacher in a diverse urban high school who was frustrated with existing curricular expectations that ignored literacy skills his students brought with them to class. His students, classified as "below average," preferred to read material related to hip-hop music and sports instead of engaging with the required text, *Julius Caesar*. Similarly, many of the student poets in Rudd's (2012) study indicated that participation in slam poetry with their fellow peers functioned as an ad hoc family for them, which was mutually supportive and affirming. However, students' engagement with spoken word poetry can also be attributed to a negative experience with identity development.

For example, when youth poets make certain truth claims about concepts such as race, gender, and sexuality, they can sometimes find themselves fenced in by their own words in a way that later feels confining (Weinstein & West, 2012). In addition to the risk of students overidentifying with the subject matter of the poems they perform, some youth poet communities may tend to create a hierarchy of artistic talent that only favors the "best" poet (Weinstein & West, 2012). Camangian (2008) suggests that a connection exists between students' engagement with spoken word poetry and their motivations to learn about artistic expression within a sociopolitical context and the development of a social justice leadership identity.

Similarly, findings from Fisher's (2005) ethnographic study of high school students' voluntary participation in after-school spoken word poetry programs suggests that students are able to force their voices and experiences out of obscurity, foster cultural awareness among each other, increase their motivation to attend school, and help them develop social relationships within an academic context. Relatedly, Wiseman (2011) investigated how the students in her eighth-grade English classroom reflected their lived experiences in their poetry. Findings from that study indicate that students in the class were exploring issues of family, personal identity, faith/religion, community, and current events and critically analyzing the perspectives of other students in the meaning-making process.

Spoken Word Poetry as Hip-Hop Pedagogy

Hip-hop is a thin stream that runs through the literature on spoken word poetry and student achievement. In the context of this chapter, I situate spoken word poetry within the foundation of rapping and emceeing in hip-hop culture that places the poet and desire for expression at the center and speaks the language of the marginalized (Smith, 2010). As English teachers in an urban high school, Morrell and Duncan-Andrade (2002) implemented hip-hop music and culture within their teaching practices to forge a common ground and critical discourse that centered on their students' lives and promoted academic literacy and critical consciousness. These authors theorized that the exploration of canonical poetry through a hip-hop lens helped their students understand the intellectual integrity, literary merit, and social critique contained within elements of their own culture.

Morrell and Duncan-Andrade (2003) expanded their theory into a qualitative study that investigated which pedagogical strategies are effective in transferring students' analytical skills of hip-hop text to canonical poetry. The authors operationalized these skills by looking for evidence of critical and analytical skills valued by K–12 and postsecondary institutions, such as uses of literary theory and terminology and willingness to deconstruct or problematize the texts. Morell and Duncan-Andrade (2003) found that positioning hip-hop as a genre of poetry was something the students were able to relate to, empowering them to see themselves as agents of critical literacy.

According to Bruce and Davis (2000), English teachers who are knowledgeable about hip-hop's cultural elements can more readily build on students' hip-hop, rap, and poetic literacies as an intervention between the structural and systemic violence that has marginalized the knowledge they bring with them to the classroom. Participants in Fisher's (2003) study indicated that hip-hop music and culture served as their motivation to move toward poetry. Hip-hop culture thrives on peer evaluation, thus preparing spoken word artists to enter a literacy-centered community where they receive feedback throughout the process of sharing the work (Fisher, 2003).

Spoken Word Poetry as Social Justice

Kinloch (2005) and Stovall (2006) make theoretical connections between spoken word poetry and social justice. Collectively, these authors posit that poetry can serve a political purpose for public school students struggling to master the convention of standard American English and academic writing. In addition, teaching social justice through poetry is a liberatory, consciousness-raising, politicized process that challenges young people to develop understandings of their world and being to engage the world as agents of change (Stovall, 2006). Valerie Kinloch served as an auxiliary English teacher who taught poetry and writing workshops to middle school students and regularly devised lesson plans that included class presentations by local poets and hip-hop artists. She encouraged her students to express themselves freely in their writing and to manipulate the "standard" way to write by adjusting their style to be congruent with language used in their lived realities, or mother tongue. Kinloch (2005) argues that meaningful, honest poetry can unveil hidden truths that can have significant implications for classroom teaching practices that involve literacy skills, creativity, and writing. These democratic engagements as a way to understand literacy are connected to reading, writing, thinking, and doing—rooted in the process and act of ideas exchange between teachers and students in an urban context (Kinloch, 2005). The students referred to in the Kinloch (2005) article "came to understand that the times they live in, we live in, are complicated by social and political struggles for power" (p. 106). Kinloch (2005) theorized that her students demonstrated access to communicative exchanges and codes that established a sense of belonging, and that reinforced their individual and collective identities.

According to Stovall (2006), an effective spoken word poetry pedagogy includes the following elements: challenging young people to think about how a poem impacts their emotions, remaining dynamic in the process of creating poetry through a consistent line of questioning that helps students develop their craft, and embracing a philosophy that performance and writing are interconnected and that to dissociate one from the other could result in a poorly constructed poem. Through a critical analysis that chronicles the experience of four spoken word artists who also serve as teacher-poets (outside of school), Stovall (2006) posits that poetry is not a means to an end, but an individual expression of responsibility to self and the human condition. From a social justice perspective, the White student poets referenced in the Stovall (2006) article came to realize that their way of life often represents the status quo, thus making it difficult for reflection. In contrast, the students of color, who rarely asked to reflect on their identity experiences, felt that engagement with spoken word poetry was transformative.

Theoretically, Watson (2013) posits that increasing racial and ethnic minority students' ability to become vocal and proud of their heritage, as well as critical of systems of oppression, could potentially bother White teachers. However, "for professional development to be successful, teachers must not feel judged for their beliefs or pedagogy, and the best tools for empowering students are also the best tools for empowering teachers" (Watson, 2013, p. 400). Are urban students of color more or less likely to have a positive response to performance poetry curriculum interventions than their White counterparts? What is culturally relevant pedagogy for White students? Is spoken word poetry an effective lens to explore critical literacy with White students? Desai and Marsh (2005) present an argument for researchers to consider critical race theory as a framework to conceptualize studies that examine the intersection of racial identities and storytelling that challenges the status quo.

Conclusion

The connection between spoken word poetry and students' academic achievement is clear. The literature discussed in this chapter places teachers at the crux of serving as the main agents for implementing spoken word poetry within their pedagogy and curriculum. There are, however, some collaborative efforts surfacing among university language arts programs, teaching poets, and English classroom interventions in urban public schools. When viewed from a historical hip-hop pedagogical lens, spoken word poetry is a form of resistance to social oppression and an opportunity to create voice and literacy agency for students of color in urban communities. A few scholars have linked spoken word poetry as an academic tool to improvements in English language learners' skill development and confidence in speaking English with fluency and full understanding. Other authors have theorized that a connection exists between antiviolence and at-risk youth interventions that use spoken word poetry as a vehicle to drive a change in behavior and an improvement in student achievement.

Ultimately, we can explore student engagement with spoken word poetry as a metaphor for a traditional classroom experience. An open mic poetry event is a classroom where the poet is the teacher and members of the audience are the students. Handwritten poems in journals, digital text on smartphones, and pages of typed print serve as course materials, and the open mic list is a canon. The topics expressed through each poem reflect a culturally relevant curriculum, and audience engagement is pedagogy. Snaps and applause are an assessment of the performance. Let us challenge ourselves to conceptualize learning as an artistic feat celebrated within the academy and responsive to the needs of diverse communities.

References

Biggs-El, C. (2012). Spreading the indigenous gospel of rap music and spoken word poetry: Critical pedagogy in the public sphere as a stratagem of empowerment and critique. *Western Journal of Black Studies, 36*(2), 161–168.

Bruce, H. E., & Davis, B. D. (2000). Slam: Hip-hop meets poetry—a strategy for violence intervention. *The English Journal, 89*(5), 119–127. doi:10.2307/822307

Camangian, P. (2008). Untempered tongues: Teaching performance poetry for social justice. *English Teaching: Practice and Critique, 7*(2), 35–55.

Desai, S. R., & Marsh, T. (2005). Weaving multiple dialects in the classroom discourse: Poetry and spoken word as a critical teaching tool. *Taboo: The Journal of Culture and Education, 9*(2), 71–90.

Fisher, M. T. (2003). Open mics and open minds: Spoken word poetry in African Diaspora Participatory Literacy Communities. *Harvard Educational Review, 73*(3), 362–389.

Fisher, M. T. (2005). From the coffee house to the schoolhouse: The promise and potential of spoken word poetry in school contexts. *English Education, 37*(2), 115–131.

Freire, P. (1970). *Pedagogy of the oppressed.* New York, NY: Continuum.

Hadaway, N. L., Vardell, S. M., & Young, T. A. (2001). Scaffolding oral language development through poetry for students learning English. *Reading Teacher, 54*(8), 796–806.

Jocson, K. M. (2005). "Taking it to the mic": Pedagogy of June Jordan's poetry for the people and partnership with an urban high school. *English Education, 37*(2), 132–148.

Kinloch, V. F. (2005). Poetry, literacy, and creativity: Fostering effective learning strategies in an urban classroom. *English Education, 37*(2), 96–114.

Lopez, A. E. (2011). Culturally relevant pedagogy and critical literacy in diverse English classrooms: A case study of a secondary English teacher's activism and agency. *English Teaching: Practice and Critique, 10*(4), 75–93.

McCormick, J. (2003). "Drag me to the asylum": Disguising and asserting identities in an urban school. *Urban Review, 35*(2), 111–28.

Morrell, E. (2005). Critical English education. *English Education, 37*(4), 312–321.

Morrell, E., & Duncan-Andrade, J. M. R. (2002). Promoting academic literacy with urban youth through engaging hip-hop culture. *The English Journal, 91*(6), 88–92. doi.org/10.2307/821822

Morrell, E., & Duncan-Andrade, J. M. R. (2003). What they do learn in school: Hip-hop as a bridge to canonical poetry. In *What They Don't Learn in School: Literacy in the Lives of Urban Youth (Vol. 2).* Retrieved from https://www.academia.edu/315032/M_What_They_Do_Learn_In_School_Hip-Hop_As_a_Bridge_to_Canonical_Poetry

Reyes, G. T. (2006). Finding the poetic high: Building a spoken word poetry community and culture of creative, caring, and critical intellectuals. *Multicultural Education, 14*(2), 10–15.

Rodriguez-Valls, F. (2009). Culturally relevant poetry: Creating *esperanza* (hope) with stanzas. *Multicultural Education, 17*(1), 11–14.

Rudd, L. L. (2012). Just "slammin!": Adolescents' construction of identity through performance poetry. *Journal of Adolescent & Adult Literacy, 55*(8), 682–691.

Smith, A. M. (2010). Poetry performances and academic identity negotiations in the literacy experiences of seventh-grade language arts students. *Reading Improvement, 47*(4), 202–218.

Stovall, D. (2006). Urban poetics: Poetry, social justice, and critical pedagogy in education. *Urban Review, 38*(1), 63–80. doi:10.1007/s11256-00

Watson, V. M. (2013). Censoring freedom: Community-based professional development and the politics of profanity. *Equity & Excellence in Education, 46*(3), 387–410.

Weinstein, S., & West, A. (2012). Call and responsibility: Critical questions for youth spoken word poetry. *Harvard Educational Review, 82*(2), 282–302.

Williams, W. R. (2015). Every voice matters: Spoken word poetry in and outside of school. *English Journal, 104*(4), 77–82.

Wiseman, A. (2010a). Family involvement in four voices: Administrator, teacher, students, and community member. *Penn GSE Perspectives on Urban Education, 7*(1), 115–124.

Wiseman, A. (2010b). "Now I believe if I write I can do anything": Using poetry to create opportunities for engagement and learning in the language arts classroom. *Journal of Language and Literacy Education, 6*(2), 22–33.

Wiseman, A. (2011). Powerful students, powerful words: Writing and learning in a poetry workshop. *Literacy, 45*(2), 70–77.

Wissman, K. (2010). "Supreme efforts of care and honest utterance": Grasping the singular power of the spoken word in school spaces. *Penn GSE Perspectives on Urban Education, 7*(2), 49–53.

Student Voices

Quay Anthony Dorsey

Alumnus, The Pennsylvania State University

Poet Self-Portrait

I was inspired to write and perform the day I saw her on stage for the first time. My mother, who's usually more shy and anxious in big crowds, started a poem by screaming, "THIS IS FOR MY SISTAS!" She went on for about three minutes describing all the beautiful and bold character traits of Black women—she even described her illness as such. She narrated her psychiatry visits through beautiful prose, and she praised the Black women who inspired her to stay strong. It was marvelous and appalling. It was as if I were watching her therapy session on stage. I was so surprised that she was so free in talking about things that were deeply personal to her and her "sistas." I looked at my mother's smile after she was done, and it was like she had the best aftertaste of her truth. I needed that in my life.

To date, my mother is still my favorite spoken word artist. When I was in my early teens, I remember our adventures in spoken word poetry very vividly. My mother competed in beauty and talent pageants for a period of her life, and poetry was always her talent. I remember standing at bus stops in the outskirts of Philly headed to Center City before the sun went down. She would spend the entire bus ride reading and practicing—practicing so loud that it should have been embarrassing. I wasn't embarrassed, but I was enthralled by her truth. My mother taught me two things through her poetry. The first thing is that a person's truth, his or her story, must be protected. Second, if your truth must be sung, make sure you're the lead singer.

I started writing with purpose during my senior year of high school. Naturally, at 17 I had the first of many "biggest life crises," and I didn't know who I was or what I was to become. My first poem, ironically, was a poem titled "This Is for My Brothers." It was an ode to Black boys who transcended the lines of normality. I read it to myself occasionally in the summer before college, but I never shared it with anyone. I guess secretly it was just an ode to boys like myself—those who wanted so bad to be heard but didn't quite know how to share. That poem was a way to help me speak my power into existence. It was a way for me to write my truth.

During my first semester of college, I found sanctuary on the ground floor of The Pennsylvania State University's student union building. I found a community I could connect with in the Paul Robeson Cultural Center. As

33

a student of color at a predominantly White institution, there were plenty of moments when I felt that I needed to feel more connected to people who looked like me. Here my poetry started to take flight because I felt part of something that was like me. I felt like I was finding my truth. I could write in my journal about being Black and gay, and there would be no assumed judgment by the White majority—which was opposite from my experience in the dorm rooms. I found time once or twice a week to go into "the Robe" to write, read, or study. I didn't talk to people much at first, but I still felt incredibly connected to them. This was my asylum, and writing in the Robe would later help improve my poetry in ways I didn't imagine.

As a child of the Robe, I made it a point to attend events they sponsored. One afternoon, I saw a flyer for an event called "Dream." The flyer had a person with a mic on it, and it looked like she was shouting something beautiful. The flyer was so reminiscent of the first time I heard my mom perform poetry. I couldn't wait to attend and listen.

I had no idea about the life-changing treat that was about to be introduced to my life. I arrived at the event early, and to my surprise there were hardly any seats. Instead there were pillows and blankets and wooden stools. The lights were dim, and the stage was dead in the center. The empty room already felt so full of good energy. Within five minutes of the show's start, the room was packed, and so was the sign-up list. When the host, Crystal Leigh Endsley, got on stage to perform an introductory poem, I knew this was the place to be. She spoke with such power and poise. Her truth and her identity as a poet were so evident to everyone in the room. I couldn't help but feel, again, that I needed this truth and identity in my life. The poets in the room that night were so connected to social justice, and their work was powerful and beautiful. After this event I wanted to write, to perform.

The Robe introduced me to two artists who help shape my work as a poet. The first was Crystal—the spitfire poet from my first open mic experience at Penn State. After my experience at "Dream," I would visit her office in the Robe and share poetry with her. She was always eager to listen and give feedback. She also inspired me to perform my work on stage the next semester. That open mic, called "Bed," led me to an invite to a group called Collective Energy. We traveled together to perform our truth at schools and open mics. The poets in this group gave me so much insight about life as an artist-activist. In my sophomore year, I met the second of the two influential artists, Tony Keith. He had taken over Crystal's position in the Robe, and like clockwork that office continued to be a stage for random open mic sessions. Tony was a bit different than Crystal, however. He not only gave me feedback but also would always stand up when I was done to read his own work. Tony and Crystal also taught me how to educate others through poetry about real issues. Each was my professor at one point or another. Not surprisingly, my work as an artist under their guidance propelled me into a career in education.

Spoken word poetry has given me a voice that I didn't know I had. As an elementary educator, it's necessary to give students the opportunity to let their voice be heard. The idea that students are bodies to be directed kills the school environment, especially while their brains and identities are developing so rapidly. Every morning, students stand up during "morning meeting" to tell their truth. Their truth is usually related to a fun activity they did on a previous day or how they are concerned about this week's lunch options. But sometimes their truth is related to their feelings on police shootings and the presidential election. Then there are times when they want to share a rap, poem, or song they wrote. All students have a story that informs who they are and what they believe.

In my life, I've seen spoken word poetry as therapy, as powerful performances, and as a tool to bridge communities. The core values of spoken word can be applied in most areas of life. No matter the form, spoken word is always full of integrity and grit. It's about community building and storytelling.

Spoken word poetry is about the truth.

Regrets

I wish I could rewind to be in your presence again
I wish I could take back what I said to you
I wish I would have spent my time with you much differently
But I couldn't. I didn't.
I did not appreciate the moments we shared
I hope you forgive my selfish ways
It was all for love I
SWEAR

At night I pray for you
For I know my actions have caused troubles in your future
I know the time we were together
I never told you how important you were to me
But YOU MATTER

And if we were to meet again
I would cherish your presence
I would use you to express love more deeply

This morning I cried at the thought of your departure
My tears of pain paint this notebook with words I didn't say to you
Images that were missed in the moment
The VOICE you NEVER heard

I took for granted your blessings
Gifts of mornings, afternoons,
and sunsets
You allowed me to breathe

I am forever grateful

You lead me to the future and remind me the past is important.
Because of you I am better than I was
Because of you I see today
And I will forever remember you,
My Yesterday

3

WORDS HAVE POWER

Spoken Word Performance as an Educational,
Community Engagement, and Personal Development
Tool for College Students

Crystal Leigh Endsley

A few months ago, I was invited to return to a campus where I formerly taught to host and execute an open mic night for the students. When I was teaching there, I founded an open mic night. There was nothing like it on campus, and it was consistently well-attended and even drew audience members from a university in a nearby town. This cultural program has been going strong for over five years now, and as we set up for the event, I wondered to myself if the open mic still served a purpose for these students. Was there still a need for a space where students could creatively express themselves voluntarily and in whatever format they wanted? Or had the new crop of students evolved past that somehow? These students populate an incredibly resourced campus, and the majority of the students of color are brought in on the Posse Foundation's scholarship program. As I began hosting the program that night, I marveled at the students still draping themselves over every possible surface to fit into the space, how they vocally expressed their appreciation for one another's work, and the nearly tangible love that settled down on us like mist. We all wanted to be there, to participate in this experience together, to witness a first-timer's poetic debut, to hear the shots fired at a recent decision by the school's administration. I was reminded of the ways that the open mic program, when served up proper, encourages and incorporates the building of a different skill set than other types of cultural programs. A program that was created out of the need, commitment, and ambition of three women of color students (shout out to Nanyamka, JR, and Tracy, who also incidentally founded the first

Feminists of Color Collective on campus because the Women's Center was excluding them) at a time when this same campus did not have a cultural center at all continued to thrive and appeal to a new generation of college students.

I had the benefit of entering my faculty position from a background that was half cultural administrator, half classroom, and all spoken word poet. I increasingly realized that my own experience occupying these spaces at the same time has benefitted my students, both in the classroom and in their campus student life. I had the privilege of observing student-artists who began to mine their scholarship to strengthen their spoken word artistry. I began to notice the increasing improvement of these same student-artists in the classrooms where I taught them in a more traditional format (Endsley, 2014). I lead here with the testimony of SpeakEasy: An Open Mic and Spoken Word Lounge, since it was my experience developing this program that positioned spoken word poetry performance by student-artists on a college campus as a trifecta of developmental tools. Community engagement; education and pedagogy; and, at the root of it all, identity development are three resulting manifestations in the lives of students when they participate regularly in an effective open mic night campus program. In my recent moment of reflection, I understood that if I could utilize my programming background as a faculty member, then I was positioned to be particularly effective. Coordinating and performing at the open mic was for me the intervention that sister-scholar Carmen Kynard and Robert Eddy (2009) articulate when they remind that "teaching in this place will mean that I have to draw from another space, be here but be from somewhere else pedagogically, politically, and historically" (p. 33). Five years in, the stream of eager student-artists and the audience members at the SpeakEasy are evidence that cultural programming which forms new and creative spaces that are otherwise considered "somewhere else," somewhere other than the college institution that is home for our students, does indeed have a lasting impact and challenges us as administrators and educators to continually invest in making our students' stories heard. At the end of this latest installment, a first-year female student of color whom I had never met approached me, introduced herself with a hug, and repeatedly thanked us for having the program. After the obligatory selfie and #speakeasy memorialized us into digital space, she asked for writing tips and a reading list and reminded me, "There is no other place like this on campus, no other event. I mean, we were all here, all listening, all really performing. I want to learn more and to participate." The open mic night provides just such an opportunity.

Bodies on the Line: Spoken Word Poetry Performance as Community Engagement

To participate in an open mic night as a student-artist is to become a member of a counterculture. The act of performance marks the difference between an audience member and a student-artist, and it is the act of performance that creates community. The degree to which spoken word poetry performance is impactful on a college campus largely hinges on performance in front of an audience. The size of the audience is irrelevant, and its response to the student-artist's performance is not necessarily a factor that determines success or failure. The most important function of live spoken word poetry performances is that they immediately crystallize the relationship between audience and performer as, first, existing, and, second, critical. Without the act of performance, it is very easy to deny any connection between the audience members and a student-artist. That artist-audience connection, that special synergy and dynamic, however, is absolutely crucial to any student or campus transformation because the relationship between audience member and performer is suddenly clarified and made real—we are each dependent on and connected to the other. A student-artist embodies that possibility while he or she is performing.

A student-artist who shares a spoken word poem invites the audience to exchange information and to create new meaning. Performance of spoken word is the negotiation of a transaction, the acknowledgment of a relationship between the audience and the student-artist. No matter the difference or disgust or desire that the artist or audience might feel toward the other, once a student-artist performs, it's undeniable that an exchange is taking place. This relationship, the trade of information, and the meaning-making that occur because of spoken word solidify the notion of performance as community and demonstrate how performance poetry can create new worlds (see Weinstein, 2009). That is the power of a live performance of spoken word poetry. That is also the danger.

To borrow the phrase of a former student and longtime friend Caty Taborda-Whitt (who is featured later in this text), recognition of the body can sometimes extend into "burdening the margins" (personal communication, C. Taborda-Whitt, April 9, 2015). Performance can go many different and unpredictable directions, rarely the same way twice. When a marginalized student performs, one who is most likely underserved and perceived as a token student of color at predominantly White institutions, the attention that focuses on their body intensifies in a space where it was already highly concentrated. Student-artists who decide to perform become "voluntarily 'socially marked,'" and their performances situate them at once as both experts and as resistors of oppressive or socially dominant narratives that pass as truth simply because narratives that benefit a majority tend to enjoy frequent circulation (Warner, 2005, p. 120). When already marginalized student-artists perform counternarratives, they are seeking to revise the discourse and also challenge the oppression and exclusion they are facing. For example, when issues of race emerge in class discussion, professors are more likely to call on students of color to explain or contribute, especially when only a few are represented in a classroom (Kynard & Eddy, 2009; Harper, 2008). Student-artists who volunteer to perform and share their spoken word, which is so often autobiographical (Fisher, 2007; Weinstein, 2009; Denzin, 2003) invite outsiders to study their experience in a narrative constructed from their own thoughts and spoken in their own voices, which can be disquieting, to say the least. Our society levels constant critique and threats of physical violence to protect against any and all sorts of protestors—peaceful or otherwise—and for students who perform, their spoken word poetry is also a protest. For students of color who are abiding on the margins of their campus and larger society to perform original and counterculture poetry that resists dominant discourses about their experiences in front of a largely hegemonic and White audience, courage must be a component of their performance. The performance experience is destabilizing and full of risks and tensions; the unknowns are part of what makes performance extremely powerful and effective as a tool of teaching and engagement. What if the audience disapproves? What if they boo? How can a college administrator ensure safety for student-artists who are already targeted and also encourage dialogue among audience members who might disagree with the performance?

Spoken word performance is the rare opportunity that creates unmitigated and unapologetic space for audience members to take responsibility for what is happening on their campus. A student-artist can introduce audience members to a world, to a social issue, to a dream or imagination that might shock, awe, and cause what we might perceive as "negative" reactions from an audience member, particularly when a poem's topic implicates the audience. When a student of color shares a personal experience of racism, for example, the audience members are required to reflect on that experience and then negotiate the meanings of their own actions. Audience members have to ask themselves if they have contributed to this experience for others. This difficult work places a high priority on reflection, and in order to be effective in this first component of community engagement, an open mic night must be uncensored, removing the barriers that restrain student-artists from communicating their experiences, hopes, and desires with agency and sovereignty. The role of student affairs administrators in maintaining safe space is "to hedge in the risk of the performance situation and enable the audience to express support for the performer. Certainly, there are varying intensities of response to each individual's performance, but there is a baseline attitude of encouragement for the very act of writing and then performing that writing in front of others" (Weinstein & West, 2012, p. 290). There are several ways to ensure that these risks are assessed and addressed without removing the necessary and celebrated vulnerability of a live poetry performance event.

Set Community Rules

The beauty and challenge of an open mic night program, much like a poetry performance, are that no two events unfold in exactly the same way. Although logistics, planning, and key players might be consistent from event to event, the performers, their poems, and the audience members always vary. To hedge in the risks while encouraging risk-taking by the student-artists, set rules that are consistent for each open mic program. These rules apply to the audience members and are not intended to censor or otherwise impact the content of the student-artists' poetry. The host of the event should open each open mic program with a reminder of the house rules, which provide consistency for the attendees, allowing them to relax into the structure of the event. This is especially helpful because the audience and the artists are new or a new combination at each, and their experience performing or participating should never be assumed. While the content of the student-artists' work can (and should!) challenge and provoke, having set expectations provides a reliable sense of security for those who are new to participating in an open mic event and eventually provides a communal way for audience members to participate and respond. House rules might vary depending on the program, but following are a few upon which I have come to rely:

- *Respect the mic.* When student-artists are on stage, the audience must show respect by not talking over them, ensuring that phone ringers are turned to vibrate, and practicing active listening.
- *One mic, one piece.* This particular rule varies depending on the size of the program and the sign-up list of the audience; however, I typically limit those students on the sign-up sheet to one piece at a time. After everyone on the sign-up sheet has been called up, and if there is time and the desire, I'll allow student-artists to return to the stage to perform a second piece. This convention encourages the artists to choose their very best piece to share and reminds the audience that their time and attention are also being respected.
- *Show love: Only positive feedback allowed.* When I host, I ask the audience to demonstrate an example of positive feedback. Typically

they respond with a hand clap, a hoot or holler, or snaps. The audience members are encouraged to give feedback, but only of the positive sort. Reminding them to listen actively and to demonstrate that by responding trains them to seek out aspects of each student-artists' performance that resonates with them. This practice of what I call *positive empathy* requires audience members to tune their ears to listen to the performance and simultaneously examine themselves for reactions they might otherwise ignore or suppress.

House rules are best introduced and enforced by the host of the open mic event. The more consistent an open mic event becomes, the more practiced the audience and student-artists become at implementing and maintaining the structure of the program themselves. Student agency and personal investment in a successful event determine the longevity of that event.

Encourage Audible Feedback

Most traditional campus classrooms make use of a system of raised hands and silent listening. One of the most unique aspects of and the appeal of an open mic night is the call-and-response that the audience is invited to vocalize throughout the night. The host should encourage the crowd to use their voices throughout the course of the event. One way to encourage audible feedback is to provide positive feedback, as described previously. Another opportunity is to pose questions to the crowd, which creates camaraderie and allows the audience members to interact with one another on a large scale, which in turn loosens them up and indicates that this is not a typical student affairs program. Between each student-artist is a window of time that can be used to casually interact with the audience and to warm them up in the practice of providing audible feedback, especially to the student-artists, most of whom will be anxious and nervous to share their work. Reminding the audience members that they are complicit in the success of the program during the actual performances keeps them engaged and also cognizant of their own responsibility to each other. Audible feedback from audience members is a critical component of creating an atmosphere of acceptance from which all members of a campus community benefit.

Debrief After Each Open Mic Event

Each cultural program deserves its own postprogram assessment. Often, such assessments are limited to written replies to questions on a worksheet or a #2 pencil bubble form that only ends up forgotten on the floor. The feedback provided on such forms doesn't always address the intrinsic moving parts of a program like an open mic and doesn't allow for tailored feedback, particularly for students who work in supporting roles for the event. Especially following an initial program, if it is new or if the student-workers are new to their positions, it is helpful to meet as a small group with the team that implements the program, highlight specific points for improvement, and emphasize what went well. Consider the following components of a debrief as a starting point.

- *Host, DJ, and student-workers.* Invite the host and DJ to share the best moments of the event with the team. Ask them what they liked best and what areas they would improve, including suggesting ways that they might encourage more audience interaction. Be sure to provide specific feedback, such as, "Your introduction of Rashida was great. The audience really responded to how you welcomed her on stage." Or you can say to a student-worker, "Thank you for making sure the sign-up list was managed. Maybe next time we can include a column for genre of performance." Keep detailed notes about each debriefing meeting as these will help when compiling year-end reports and in tracking progress for the program and for student-worker annual evaluations.
- *Collaborators and cosponsors.* The student organizations that may cosign to support an open mic program might express different sorts of expectations for the event. The participation they provide is helpful, and I've often found that including their skill-set and promoting their events ensures buy-in to attending an event they've either funded or for which they've provided in-kind support. Communicate objectives, expectations, and outcomes with each collaborator after a program ends. If the cosponsor was departmental, then perhaps a written letter providing some of the figures (attendance, outcome, number of performers) is satisfactory. Be sure to include future ideas for growth if you anticipate executing the program again. If the program was a means to groom student leaders in the art of collaboration, then I suggest an in-person meeting that invites their feedback and encourages them to expand their constituents' investment and level of participation.
- *Don't forget virtual participation as an assessment tool.* In the digital age, hashtags, Snapchats, and Facebook Live streams are important tools of assessment that won't be reflected in a worksheet evaluation. Ensure that none of this virtual feedback is discounted, and assign a student-worker to organize the figures based on numbers of likes, comments, views, and posts. Consider uploading an online survey for students

to complete about the program, and always be sure to encourage the use of a central hashtag to streamline the photos afterward. You never know when an audience member will capture a great shot that otherwise would be missed.

Conducting a debriefing is a critical practice of self-reflection found in the strongest pedagogical and programming practices (Harper and Quaye, 2007). Debriefing after an open mic program is crucial for the student-artist as well, and unfortunately this aspect of the open mic is often undervalued and underestimated. This component of the open mic night absolutely cannot be compromised. Self-reflexivity is an integral exercise paramount to the success of any creative or intellectual artistic endeavor and as such requires that any actor in the program must reflect upon his or her own participation and include those observations in the final work (see Brown, 2013). In other words, the debrief that follows the execution of a program plays a role as part of the performance *and* community engagement. Part of demonstrating support and offering validation to college student-artists extends before and after the performance of spoken word poetry, and modeling how to conduct these sorts of postprogram reviews reminds students that self-reflection practice is a tool of effectiveness and success.

"I Am Whatever You Say I Am": Spoken Word Poetry as Identity Development

The stage and open mic are crucial elements of identity development for the emerging college student-artist. Behind the stage's curtain, so to speak, remains another element that is just as foundational and perhaps more crucial, because without it, the performance won't happen at all: writing and rehearsing. "Spoken word performance provides a way to be seen and heard for students whose concerns, lives, dreams are often unheeded," and yet there is the ongoing work of writing a poem and then revising that poem that must be attended to prior to the performance itself (Endsley, 2016, p. 20). What the stage elevates in a public performance is actually the result of behind-the-scenes work that most often occurs in solitude. The centrality of identity and culture to spoken word poems are both the cause and effect of the performance; student-artists as well as audience members experience a heightened awareness of the body because the act of performance is tied up with the fact that most artists' initial work is rooted in introspective reflection based on their own identities (Jocson, 2008). The level of impact possible for marginalized student-artists' spoken word performance is amplified by their movement through discourses about their identities. For a marginalized student on campus to move in one performance from border to center stage is a dramatic shift, and what happens when that student shifts back to the border after the open mic program? It takes more than one stellar performance for a campus life audience to reflect the work that goes on during an open mic, and the student-artist might not be prepared for any new sense of offstage notoriety.

Realizing who we are and are not is a process, and a very public one at that. Through community we learn and teach what is acceptable and what is forbidden, what is sacred and what is commonplace (Thiong'o, 1997). The relationship between artist and the audience is a communal one, a very concentrated type of community, not based solely on geography or on racial or gender identity, but drawn together because of praxis. The identity, geographic location, and power(lessness) of a student-artist are tightly tied together, and these factors are highly varied depending on the campus (Giroux & McLaren, 1992). Living and writing from these margins make the open mic and the stage a highly contested space that complicates even as it offers clarity and empowerment. The open mic offers the rare moment on the stage that validates the stories and ideas of student-artists even as it values the feedback of their peers. The complexities of any one aspect of a student-artists' identity, and the performance of that identity, can be extracted and interrogated through performance, which is both empowering and devastating. Student-artists are enabled to grow and learn more about themselves and the "world they imagine" while also being measured and found wanting by an audience (Denzin, 2003, p. 129). Spoken word poetry and performance are integral tools for student-artists' personal development and exploration of their own intersecting identities. Student-artists who can first position themselves are better equipped to learn about others (Endsley, 2016).

Performing spoken word poetry in front of an audience moves the student-artist beyond creating an individual, solitary piece of art and solo written narrative. Performance breaks the notion that any one story or experience occurs or is created outside of a social context and location that involves historical, geographical, economical, and political influences and structures. This context urgently incorporates the audience of the poem and immediately brings the social position of the student-artist to bear on the campus. Performance insists that a collective of voices is being heard, in conversation with each other and in dialogue with the audience. Performance shoves student-artists into communication with their peers, breaking the walls of confinement so often experienced by exceptional marginalized students. In this way, open mic night insistently maintains community-building as a central outcome of spoken word poetry performance and provides connections between the students' isolated experience and the world around them.

The community that is built, however, is made up of different voices, experiences, and youth who are in the midst of struggling to find out or express who they are. These individuals are publicly exploring parts of their lives that often trouble them, that worry and hang them up like a ragged fingernail on the threads of a garment. The performance of spoken word poetry thus begins as an individual process, a moment of pause and internal reflection through writing. Open mic night provides a second point of reflection, an opportunity for the student-artist to look up and outward, to check for external signs of recognition in the audience, to listen for feedback that acknowledges their work and pain and hope.

After the performance of a spoken word poem, the student-artist has the opportunity to revise, rework, and rehearse the performance; to gauge its effectiveness; to review the objectives for the poem. The act of performance might catapult that student into a totally new role on campus, or it might simply provide a platform for continuing on a path to self-discovery. For other student-artists, the stakes are not quite as high. The opportunity to perform is a way to audition a new mode of living or thinking, to challenge an idea without committing their life "offstage" to a cause. Sometimes performance is a way to communicate desires that a student-artist is uncomfortable with, wants he or she might later shrug off as "just a poem" or name as a performance, and therefore "not a big deal."

On the other hand, the student-artists who choose to perform poems that are intensely personal and position the artist as deeply vulnerable—especially more than once in front of their peers—are exercising what I name *rehearsal of representation.* Such performances are moments of creative and energetic auditioning of new or more complex identity performances that a student-artist desires to enact more regularly in his or her day-to-day life on campus. Open mic night is a stage that offers a space to audition a new portrayal of themselves or a new, revised reading of an aspect of their identity within the confines of the stage. If the house rules are in place, then they can be assured that no one will boo them off the stage. At the same time, student-artists can test the waters of a developing identity or of rejecting a past trauma, and audition a new meaning for a stale issue they have faced. They are rehearsing a new way to represent themselves to the world, to their peers, and to themselves.

Even if your office or center does not have the resources to create a new small-scale program, there are opportunities for support that might be offered to student-artists who are rehearsing a new representation of themselves. One option is to establish an intentional relationship with student-artists as you do with student leaders. This might mean debriefing with the student-artists who perform. Perhaps you don't have an established relationship with the student-artists who perform in the same way that you might interact with the student-workers who assist in your office. Is it possible to collect the e-mail addresses of the students who sign up to perform? Follow up with a personal e-mail to them after the open mic night, encouraging them to continue attending and performing. Add them to your mailing list and find time to meet and ask them for their input about the program.

Another critical strategy to better support student-artists is to connect your resources. If there aren't resources to support a small-scale student-artist development program (see Endsley, 2016), then consider the possible connections that you might be able to make for student-artists with other departments. Reach out to the English department or writing center on your campus and see if either hosts workshops for creative writing. Is there a slam poetry student organization on campus? Link the student-artists with them for potential future collaborations. Sometimes the best way to recruit and retain marginalized students is through cultural programming, and the invitation to participate in support services or future programs appeals to a holistic sense of well-being for these students.

Open mic night so often requires collaboration across departments and partnerships with student organizations. Collaboration can translate in many ways, such as sharing funds, networks, and the logistical duties associated with every successful program. Transforming a campus location that is familiar to the student body into a safe space for creating and sharing what is often intimately personal experience requires shifting the atmosphere. Expanding these components is central to supporting student-artists consistently, beyond having a great time at a campus program. Approaching an open mic night from the perspectives outlined in this chapter will facilitate student-artists as they develop their identity and the critical community with other student-artists. Working in tandem, community engagement and the nurturing of identity development are essential components that strengthen the case for consistent, committed open mic night programs on college campuses.

References

Brown, R. N. (2013). *Hear our truths: The creative potential of Black girlhood.* Urbana, IL: University of Illinois Press.

Denzin, N. K. (2003). *Performance ethnography: Critical pedagogy and the politics of culture.* Thousand Oaks, CA: Sage.

Endsley, C. L. (2014). Performing blackness: Spoken word poetry and performance. *Transformations: Journal of Inclusive Scholarship and Pedagogy, 34*(1–2), 110–120.

Endsley, C. L. (2016). *The fifth element: Social justice pedagogy through spoken word poetry.* Albany, NY: SUNY Press.

Fisher, M. (2007). *Writing in rhythm: Spoken word poetry in urban classrooms.* New York, NY: Teachers College Press.

Giroux, H., & McLaren, P. (1992). Writing from the margins: Geographies of identity, pedagogy, and power. *The Journal of Education, 174*(1), 7–30.

Harper, S. (2008). *Creating inclusive campus environments: For cross-cultural learning and student engagement.* Boston, MA: NASPA.

Harper, S., & Quaye, S. J. (2007). Student organizations as venues for Black identity expression and development among African American male student leaders. *Journal of College Student Development, 48*(2), 127–144.

Jocson, K. (2008). *Youth poets: Empowering literacies in and out of schools.* New York, NY: Peter Lang.

Kynard, C., & Eddy, R. (2009). Toward a new critical framework: Color-conscious political morality and pedagogy at historically Black and historically White colleges and universities. *College Composition and Communication, 61*(1), W24–W44.

Thiong' o N. (1997). Enactments of power: The politics of performance space. *The Drama Review, 41*, 11–30.

Warner, M. (2005). *Publics and counterpublics.* Brooklyn, NY: Zone Books.

Weinstein, S. (2009). *Feel these words: Writing in the lives of urban youth.* Albany, NY: SUNY Press.

Weinstein, S., & West, A. (2012). "Call and responsibility: Critical questions for youth spoken word poetry." *Harvard Educational Review, 82*(2), 282–302.

Student Voices

Caty Taborda-Whitt

Alumna, Hamilton College

Poet Self-Portrait

As a first-generation student, I didn't have any sort of road map or model for attending college. Like most undergraduates, I was both anxious and excited to learn new things, meet new people, and grow. But unlike many of my peers, it became increasingly clear that higher education was never designed with people like me in mind. First-generation. Latina. Working-class. Child of an immigrant. I sought community and support from others who might relate to my experiences, but it wasn't always easy to find, especially in campus programming.

Like many college campuses, mine often hosted artistic showcases or open mic nights, but they were mostly geared toward aspiring acoustic songwriters, a cappella groups, or the occasional improv comedy troupe. These performances were entertaining, but I never personally felt passionate or connected to these programs. They didn't cater to or include voices from the margins. The absence of visible faces or stories like mine only reinforced the long history of institutes of higher education excluding marginalized students. Even now in an era when universities are changing admission policies, financial aid packages, and course offerings to correct these histories, many campuses still struggle to create cultural spaces that make diverse experiences and identities visible.

I found spoken word late in my college career. A newly hired Africana studies professor arrived during my senior year, bringing with her over 10 years of experience in campus organizing and spoken word performance. I first met Crystal Leigh Endsley at a Women's Center meeting. This was odd, given that professors rarely came to student organization meetings, let alone introduced themselves and offered support. She brought with her a list of potential projects, but most notably she proposed a multiorganization collaboration to host a "SpeakEasy" open mic night featuring spoken word poetry.

"A what?" we asked.

Shocked that we had never seen any sort of campus spoken word performance, she described cozy floor seating, a visual arts showcase, a DJ, and professional hosts. I could hardly visualize it, but nonetheless I jumped at the chance to assist with the event.

During the weeks leading up to the first-ever SpeakEasy, Crystal and I met often to discuss logistics. Amid space design and advertising campaigns,

I toyed with the idea of performing. I had never shared my writing before, let alone performed anything on campus. To me the stage seemed lonely, just a mic and your words, and each time I considered it, I quickly dismissed myself as unqualified. *Besides*, I thought, *what if I'm not good? What if nobody liked it?* Yet I wrote for hours each day, sequestered in my dorm room, thinking about all the things I wished I had the courage to share. Finally, the day before the SpeakEasy, I committed.

I can still feel the anxious twinge that permeated my gut hours before the SpeakEasy even began. As the performance lounge filled to the brim with enthusiastic audience members—a much larger crowd than we could have ever anticipated—I started to worry that all of my fears of embarrassment and isolation would be realized. I'd be alone up there on that stage, out of my league among the slew of other student performers who had a knack for creative writing and the confidence to perform. But before I could talk myself out of it, I heard the DJ call my name to the stage.

The performance was uncomfortable at times. Slow to start, I stumbled over my words as I anxiously read from the crinkled paper clenched between my hands. But with each deep breath, I kept reading, until finally I heard a cheer. I looked up and no longer felt alone with a microphone; instead, I saw my community. Some were friends, but more surprisingly, many of the supportive cheers came from people I didn't know. I gained momentum, becoming less dependent on the paper and instead feeding off the energy of the crowd. The live feedback was exhilarating. Unexpectedly, my words—four years' worth of pent-up frustrations about what it felt like to be a first-generation student of color—struck a chord. For weeks after the SpeakEasy, people I had never spoken to in my three previous years of college suddenly approached me to talk about my poem. Even people who hadn't been in attendance had heard about it and wanted to discuss it. Let me be very clear: this wasn't because I am a particularly great performer or talented poet. But for that one night at least, I didn't hold back, and my words resonated with others.

I learned two things from that first SpeakEasy. First, I am braver than I knew. Second, performance is community. By its very nature, a spoken word poetry night is interactive and demands a relationship between the performer and the audience. This relationship extends beyond the performance itself, opening up a new avenue for community building. For me, performing meant that I had a space to express ideas, feelings, and experiences that I never had the means to express before, and it also provided a space for audience members to learn about their peers. Students who had never spoken during class or organization meetings suddenly took the stage. Without knowing it, the SpeakEasy was what we had been waiting for, and it has since become an annual tradition at that college.

Spoken word performance provides a critical opportunity for community building on college campuses, especially for otherwise marginalized students who often struggle to find one another. Though accessible to everyone, spoken word's roots in hip-hop and social justice provide a space ripe for supporting and empowering communities of color. That first SpeakEasy was the first time in my four years of college that I saw a room filled with so many other faces of color. Students and faculty of different ages, backgrounds, and social circles attended. Some professors even brought their young children so that they, too, could hear and see what community could look like for them.

I find it ironic that I once saw the stage as lonely. Spoken word poetry is anything but isolating. It brings together people from all corners of campus and sparks conversations that last well beyond performance night. The weeks leading up to performances are filled with planning meetings between organizations and groups that may otherwise never collaborate. Even writing itself becomes an opportunity to gather, as many of us met days before performance night to run ideas and lines past one another. I am grateful that I found spoken word as a college student and only wish I had found it sooner.

Excerpt From My First Open Mic Night

Ethnicity is not something to be proved for fearing losing it
And race is not a card you can revoke like a ticket
So regardless of whether or not I "look it"
I undoubtedly carry the weight of those that came before me
No matter how many census boxes I check
It does not mean you know me personally

And by now I've grown to used
To that confused look on those faces
Of people trying to figure which 3rd world
Crossed the 1st world
To create this 2nd generation of mixed races
Should I be so lucky then he and I could trade places
So that for one day he too could stomach the shame
Of being erased from history's pages

I've grown resentful of whoever's decision it was
To make these incisions among the whole human race
And with such poor precision that these divisions
Locked us into boxes for too long

4

TALKING BACK AND MOUTHING OFF

The Importance of Privileging Student Voice in Student Affairs Programming

Toby S. Jenkins

Places of Possibility

In the classic story *The Wonderful Wizard of Oz* (Baum, 1900), the young character, Dorothy, is swept up in a storm and taken away to a foreign and sometimes frightening land. Dorothy spends the length of the story searching for a sense of belonging, for home. Along the way, she meets other abandoned souls— those who are also looking for someone to simply help. As a collective, they are in search of a wizard to work his magic and meet their unique needs. They are searching for Oz. In many ways, this story mirrors the educational experience for some women students in the science, technology, engineering, and math (STEM) arena. With the field of higher education continuing to face serious challenges with issues of admission, retention, and completion for all students of color, many wounded learners are in need of alternative places of inclusion and creative educators who can work their magic so that these learners are truly engaged and included (Harper, Patton, & Wooden, 2009; hooks, 2003; Hurtado, 1992; Lambert, Terenzini, & Lattuca, 2007; Lopez, 1993; Rendón, Jalomo, & Nora, 2004). Part of the problem is that in our attempts to transform education, we actually stand still. We continue to examine the same spaces to better understand their faults and problems rather than taking a creative and inspiring journey (the yellow brick road) toward new and fresh perspectives. We focus on pathology rather than possibility.

What possibilities do the places and spaces of cultural inclusion outside of the perimeters of traditional educational institutions hold? How is it that our music, our streets, our homes, and our folkways continue to successfully pull and attract students in deep and meaningful ways? These nontraditional spaces of education are in many ways the real-world manifestation of the fictional Oz. Metaphorically, Oz is a space of belonging. It is welcoming—a place the nonconformists can call "home," where Munchkins and fairies are treated like kings and queens. It is different and a bit unorthodox, but it works. We should all be searching for Oz, for places of possibility, creative imagination, and cultural inclusion. Though many researchers and education activists have championed the inclusion of students' cultures into the college experience—and many resources such as cultural centers, multicultural affairs departments, and ethnic studies departments were established as a result of this work—the overall college experience is still one that in many ways separates a student from his or her cultural community. So, if culture is critical to students coming from current or historically oppressed communities, why is there often such limited space in college for an education that puts student culture and voice at the center?

Privileging Student Voice

Over 20 years ago, Baxter Magolda (1992) offered research and learning principles that called for educators to validate students as knowers and to situate learning in the students' lived experience. Two decades later it is still important to state directly the need for educators to relinquish formal notions of power and invite students to share their perspectives as experts of their own experience. Privileging student voice is an important aspect of transformational pedagogy. As a former student affairs practitioner, I firmly believe that student affairs professionals are educators outside of the classroom. How practitioners structure campus programs and events in order to educate, train, and develop college students is a form of pedagogy. Moreover, the use of performance, storytelling, and critical voice in cocurricular programming represents the development of a critical pedagogy of humanism (pedagogy rooted in the students' lived experience). A critical pedagogy of imagination and humanism concerns creating educational spaces where the educational content matters to students.

Imagination embodies voice, consciousness, community, pluralism, and the human condition. A critical pedagogy opens up spaces for imaginative possibilities and a caring, unconditional dialogue within the bureaucracy of schooling. The invigorating spaces of imagination also provide learners with the capacity to reach beyond conventional ideology to engage in free, unpredictable, and internalized thought, while also building on lived experience (Rautins & Ibrahim, 2011).

Beyond allowing students to speak their own truths, spoken word culture broadly acknowledges the validity and importance of the act of storytelling (truth telling, speaking out, oppositional thinking, bearing witness, and remembering) as culture, art, education, and political activism. In many ways, to create an open, honest, and critical dialogue on a college campus is quite transformative. Though the popular imagining of *college* often paints it as an experience rich with debate, heated exchange, and philosophical questioning, too often college campuses have become spaces of compliance. Certain behaviors are rewarded, and others are punished, which raises important questions regarding privilege on college campuses. Who has the space to think and reflect on their experience (in this case, who gets to go to college and have the privilege of spending four years as a thinker/learner)? In what spaces are college student voices allowed to speak (e.g., solely in classrooms or throughout and beyond campus)? How do space and environment determine how you can speak (the language you can use and how loud you can yell)? In other words, is it okay to yell your oppositional thinking in a classroom but not appropriate to do so in the main administration building? Questioning and criticizing the administration is typically not viewed as rich critical thinking and necessary dialogue for institutional change. It is viewed as campus unrest, and the response is to strategize on how to silence student protestors. We often view student protest as a disruption to campus order and a disrespectful form of talking back.

As an African American woman scholar, I know that space is only transformed when it is disrupted, and so I look back into my cultural life and place new value and meaning on the concept of *talking back*. Talking back was something that well-behaved children didn't do. Talking back was a form of disrespect, but it might depend on to whom you were talking. When examining the conditions of the world, the ways that many populations are oppressed, and the social systems that sustain such oppression, talking back becomes a necessary form of oppositional thinking. So we encourage our students to talk back and mouth off to society—to give voice to the voiceless and speak an unflinching truth through their written and spoken works. Great oppositional thinkers have pushed to expand our laws, our behavior, and our opinions, and artists have been some of our most public and resistant voices. In a direct and unapologetic manner, artists creatively give voice to the unique experiences and perspectives of the marginalized and oppressed. This is why art is an important platform for college student activism.

Ultimately, in any type of educational experience we are creating spaces for students to work through critical issues. Culturally rich educational experiences should offer healthy, affirming, and safe arenas in which students can effectively explore the issues most relevant in their lives. Essentially, the idea of creating safe spaces is truly about creating environments in which risk-taking, deep exploration, controversy, and complexity can be engaged, embraced, and appreciated rather than feared and avoided. *Safe* does not necessarily mean *comfortable*, but it does imply a valuable opportunity for healthy growth—pushing, pulling, nurturing, challenging, and affirming.

Art as a Form of Cultural Leadership

One cannot explore the ways in which culture influences activism and resistance without considering factors such as race, class, and gender. Understanding how cultural hegemony impedes the healthy growth and appreciation of cultures that have been placed on the margins of society helps us to visualize the type of leadership ethic that is needed to resist cultural hegemony. Feminist theory considers cultural hegemony to be a social system that involves devaluing nondominant cultures. Hegemony and cultural imperialism concern the domination of power; one social class or entity has power over the other. Beyond the ways that this power of dominion provides the dominant group access to resources, wealth, and opportunity, this group's values, behaviors, beliefs, and ways of knowing and being become the norm. In the case of leadership, the bold and visionary work of many members within marginalized communities is often overlooked and not included in traditional ideologies of leadership. Additionally, the college experience is often predicated on a sense of delayed gratification: at the end of the experience you get a job, you are on your own, and you are viewed as an official adult—*at the end*. Quality education in college offers students opportunities to create, envision, advocate, develop, serve, and affect the world while they are in college. When students are exposed to real issues, engage with real communities, and are encouraged to develop a strong voice while they are in the act of "becoming," who they eventually become might forever be changed.

Ultimately, I view the artistic work that college students produce at campus open mics as a form of cultural leadership. A leadership proxy that is centered in culture and based on resistance and that engages creative strategies to privilege the minds of the marginalized is critical to how I have defined the concept of *cultural leadership*. In my book *My Color, My Culture, My Self: Heritage, Resilience, and Community Among Young Adults* (Jenkins, 2013), I share the following five components of cultural leadership:

1. An understanding of the cultural self: Cultural leaders are constantly exploring and deepening their understanding of their cultural values, beliefs, and ideologies. Cultural leaders are reflective, wise, and holistic leaders who understand that the collective of their life experiences—in the classroom or on the block, in college or in church, through professional networks or through dysfunctional family trees—have made them who they are.

2. A use of culture as a leadership tool: Cultural leadership draws on things like the cultural arts, family/community fellowship, spirituality, and other creative forms of expression to create social change. Cultural leadership values the potential of culture to serve as a community education tool to teach politics of survival, and to create a space for dialogue, discussion, action, and change.

3. A value for servitude: Like the family, community, or village that grooms culture, cultural leadership is a selfless act. Cultural leaders understand that leadership is not about hierarchy, position, or top-down structures.

4. A sense of community love and rootedness: Cultural leaders are rooted in the community (to both the people and the land) in such a way that they don't feel like an outsiders even if they are. Ultimately, this deep connection, commitment, and loyalty to a community are rooted in love. Cultural leaders are driven by an ethic of love—a love for people, a love for justice, and the hope for all people to not only experience equality (equality allows for basic needs to be accessed and met) but more importantly to experience a life filled with joy and love (which is a higher state of being).

5. A critical lens: Navigating the world when you are a part of an underrepresented cultural group often causes you to view that world a bit differently. The lived experience of underrepresented ethnic groups have taught us that an important change is made when we turn a critical eye towards social norms, laws, values, and behaviors. We must embrace the art of questioning. Cultural leadership compels us to voice and act on our criticisms in an effort to make our world more inclusive, democratic, and free. (p. 159).

In the 1970s, James Macgregor Burns was one of the first to revise the idea of leadership from a focus on "transactions" to a focus on "transformation" (Burns, 1982). More recently, in the book *Exploring Leadership*, Komives, Lucas, and McMahon (2007) stress the understanding of leadership as "a relational process of people coming together to accomplish change or make a difference to benefit the common good" (p. 91). These perspectives that have worked to expand the conversation on leadership beyond the individual and toward the collective, beyond position and toward purpose, and beyond organizational management and toward social and global change have helped us understand what quality leadership actually looks like.

These theories not only explain how groups and organizations need to function in order to effectively create change but also remind us that the decisions everyday people make in their lives—the neighborhoods they move into, the companies for which they work, the groceries they buy, or the community-based activities in which they participate—are all forms of leadership that can have an important social impact on others. The existing scholarship on leadership has led us in important and insightful directions. But are there additional sources to consult that might give us a fuller portrait— that might deepen our appreciation and understanding of what culture, leadership, and leadership scholarship should look like? Culture and leadership have lived in towns, villages, shacks, and shanties long before they lived in books, retreats, training programs, and conferences. Learning about how culture intersects with leadership requires us to look beyond textbooks and classrooms and to reconsider what knowledge should shape our understanding.

Art in Social Action

The spoken word programs that I have created on several college campuses (University of Maryland; the Pennsylvania State University; University of Hawai'i; and Georgia Southern University) were designed in direct response to the growing need to develop both critical art consumers and performers in a society dominated by popular culture. Many of America's youth are over-whelmed by depictions in the media, film, magazines, and music videos that drive and influence beliefs regarding an authentic representation of a popu-lation's culture. The programs were driven by Mulana Karenga's theory of social artistic responsibility. According to Karenga (2005), socially responsible artistic expression must meet the following qualifications: It must be (a) func-tional, possessing the ability to address social issues, particularly those affecting oppressed and marginalized communities; (b) collective, representing the full-ness of the cultural experience of a people; and (c) committing, offering forth a motivation for the realization of a people's true potential and an active work against social limitations. Not taking these criteria too literally, essentially I appreciate the foundation that underscores his philosophy. If you are given a microphone, use it to talk about something meaningful. In many ways, art and performance spaces are the only arenas in which impoverished, disenfran-chised, racially oppressed people are allowed to speak—given a microphone with the entire world listening. I agree with the belief that we should encourage our artists to make that opportunity matter. It makes sense to feel this way about art spaces in educational settings. But what about within the larger popular culture? Popular culture is the mechanism that most widely exposes young people to art.

As shared in earlier chapters of this book, spoken word has grown in popularity and become a major publicly accessible form of artistic expression. Through the many spoken word lounges in major cities, the HBO *Def Poetry Jam* and *Brave New Voices* series, and the numerous open mic events on college campuses across the country, spoken word has become both popular and commercialized. However, as an art form, it continues to hold weight as a grassroots and authentic means of social expression. Through spoken word, public and community-based artists are able to fully and honestly give voice to relevant local or global issues in ways not offered through traditional media venues.

Within the media, non-White racial groups remain underrepresented in terms of employment and are frequently represented with stereotypical images across the programming spectrum from entertainment to the nightly news. Consumers should understand that popular culture represents a major source of information about various cultures to audiences around the world. Data indicate that in television drama, women are outnumbered by men three to one, and in soap operas they are outnumbered seven to three (Ingham, 1995). Even in children's television, males dominate by 70% to 85% (Ingham, 1995). This makes leveraging access to more balanced art forms and ideas a priority for organizations like colleges and universities that are dedicated to meaningful cultural production. For our nation to continue toward its goal of becoming a truly open and democratic society, future social leaders and artists must be encouraged to understand how the content of art and entertainment influences attitudes, beliefs, and ideas.

Creating a Space for Student Voice and Activism in Practice

Young adults need to be encouraged to see the power in their lived experiences, their perspectives, and ultimately their voices. Within the campus-based cultural programs that I have created, this has meant resisting the traditional practice of bringing national speakers, thinkers, and lecturers to educate our campus community and instead offering students or recent college graduates an opportunity to engage this role. In 2005 I created a Cultural Practitioner in Residence (CPIR) program at Penn State University. The basic concept was to provide a short-term residency within our cultural center for a newly minted college graduate whose professional interest was to become a community educator, artist, or writer. These are the career paths our parents often cringe at hearing that we are interested in taking. It's a difficult road to make a viable living as a "community artist" or "community educator." But I believe that a pursuit of passion breeds success, so we began to offer a space for young people to give their passion some shape—to give them an extended opportunity on a college campus to not just pursue a degree but to map out their life purpose.

Our first CPIR was Jason Reynolds. Jason was a former student of mine from the University of Maryland. He was serious about becoming a working author—not writing books part-time. He wanted to live a life as a full-time author. Jason was an incredible writer and an amazing spoken word artist. He was one of the most popular student poets on the University of Maryland campus. As I drafted the conceptual outline for this program, I immediately thought of him. *What's Jason doing right now? How is it going for him?* We brought Jason as our first CPIR, and he spent a very short week with us on campus—a visit packed with experiences. At one point, he looked so tired that I asked him how he was holding up. He responded that he was worn out, but even that was a good experience. If he wanted to do this for a living, he needed to build up the stamina to be on tour, constantly performing, constantly participating in discussions and interviews. It was a good snapshot of what was to come.

During the week Jason served as a guest lecturer for a few English courses; he facilitated a poetry workshop at our campus daycare for three- to four-year-olds (tough crowd); he participated in networking lunches and conversations with university professors who had carved out viable careers as successful authors and artists; he served as the feature poet at our campus spoken word lounge and shared the stage with The Roots emcee Black Thought; and finally he served as a panelist at a major program called Lyrical Legacies. Lyrical Legacies brought together elders Amiri Baraka and Sonia Sanchez together with younger poets Ursula Rucker and Jason Reynolds to have a multigenerational conversation about poetry as a tool of social action. Jason found himself on stage with two writing giants, giving his own opinions and perspectives on the issue. After each question or dialogue, one poet took the mic to perform a poem. The two poets who brought the house down with ovation were Amiri Baraka and Jason Reynolds. His voice was appreciated and applauded.

As an arts administrator, I understood the value of encouraging young adults to learn from their elders, but I also understood that it would take a creative approach to campus programming in order to get students there. Jason was the featured poet at our very first spoken word lounge on campus.

To attract students, I booked Black Thought as the other feature. This was Pennsylvania and everybody loves The Roots. The event went over capacity. But what was interesting is that once again, although the celebrity head-liner was, of course, loved and adored as he recited verses from his songs a cappella, it was Jason who brought down the house with his poetry and really sparked an energy and excitement for spoken word that would eventually make this program one of the most successful on campus. I know for sure that leveraging the voices of young adults has been critical to the success of my programs.

Our program Collective Energy was born out of student need. As our spoken word lounge became increasingly popular, more and more students were interested in trying their hand at writing and performing. This was a great response, but eventually it became overwhelming when students were continually coming into our offices to share their poems. We embraced an open-door policy for students, but at some point we did have a department to run and programs to plan. We couldn't sit and listen to poetry all day, as much as we would have liked to. So, one night as I was watching a documentary on the Harlem Renaissance that explored the writing circles that were created by Langston Hughes and Zora Neale Hurston, I began to consider providing this same type of structured experience for our students. They clearly wanted guidance from us as they experimented with spoken word, and so we developed an integrated arts seminar that would allow budding campus poets, singers, and even instrumentalists to gather with us once a week to develop their work, engage in a writing support circle, and develop collaborative performances that integrated music and spoken word. Collective Energy was born.

This group became our regular feature at our campus open mic. We also took them on local and regional tours to perform at the state prison and public schools in Washington DC. Finally, we took this group on an Art in Social Action alternative spring break, visiting the University of the West Indies–Trinidad and Tobago to explore the use of spoken word as a community education tool in the West Indies. In this experience, my staff and I were simply guides and colearners. We facilitated discussions, but we also wrote and performed as poets ourselves. I created collaborative pieces with undergraduate students, acknowledging our shared and equal space as artists. Much later, my former graduate assistant who coordinated the program used the program as the subject of study for her dissertation. As I read her research, she pointed out that my willingness to partner with undergrads on spoken word pieces boosted their confidence as scholars, professionals, and artists—to perform with a university administrator and department head was meaningful to the students. I never considered this aspect of the program.

Relinquishing power or the role of expert was easy. I was motivated to partner with students because I saw their minds and their voices as being simply beautiful.

References

Baum, L. Frank. (1900). *The Wonderful Wizard of Oz*. Chicago, IL: George M. Hill Company.

Baxter Magolda, M. B. (1992). *Knowing and reasoning in college: Gender-related patterns in student intellectual development*. San Francisco, CA: Jossey-Bass.

Burns, J. M. (1982). *Leadership*. New York, NY: Harper Perennial.

Harper, S. R., Patton, L. D., & Wooden, O. S. (2009). Access and equity for African American students in higher education: A critical race historical analysis of policy efforts. *Journal of Higher Education, 80*(4), 389–414.

hooks, b. (2003). *Teaching community: A pedagogy of hope*. New York, NY: Routledge.

Hurtado, S. (1992). The campus racial climate. *The Journal of Higher Education, 63*(5), 539–569.

Ingham, H. (1995). The portrayal of women on television. Retrieved from https://www.scribd.com/document/48834397/The-Portrayal-of-Women-on-Television

Jenkins, T. (2013). *My culture, my color, my self: Heritage, resilience, and community among young adults*. Philadelphia, PA: Temple University Press.

Karenga, M. (2005). *Kwanzaa: A celebration of family, community and culture. Commemorative Edition*. Los Angeles, CA: University of Sankore Press.

Komives, S., Lucas, N., & McMahon, T. (2007). *Exploring leadership: For college students who want to make a difference*. San Francisco, CA: Jossey Bass.

Lambert, A. D., Terenzini, P. T., & Lattuca, L. R. (2007). More than meets the eye: Curricular and programmatic effects on student learning. *Research in Higher Education, 48*(2), 141–168.

Lopez, G. E. (1993). *The effect of group contact and curriculum on White, Asian American, and African American students' attitudes*. Doctoral dissertation, University of Michigan.

Rautins, C., & Ibrahim, A. (2011). Wide-awakeness: Toward a critical pedagogy of imagination, humanism, agency, and becoming. *International Journal of Critical Pedagogy, 3*(3), 12–33.

Rendón, L., Jalomo, R., and Nora, A. (2004). Theoretical considerations in the study of minority student retention in higher education. In J. M. Braxton (Ed.), *Reworking the student departure puzzle* (pp. 87–106). Nashville, TN: Vanderbilt University Press.

Student Voices

Opeyemi Owoeye (O-Slice)

Student, University of Maryland

Poet Self-Portrait

I first fell in love with spoken word in middle school. I was already head over heels for rap, but I stumbled upon some slam poetry videos on You-Tube, and the emotional connection that the poets could make me feel, even through video, was profound. Spoken word affected my college experience for two reasons. First, it allowed me to elevate my performances. Often when I got tired of performing my songs the same way, I would perform them as spoken word pieces. This allowed me dictate the flow and tempo of a piece while putting emphasis on the parts that I really wanted the audience to understand. Second, when school and life felt overwhelming, I used spoken word as a stress reliever. I attended Juke Joint every month and open mics in Washington DC once a week. I enjoyed attending open mics because there was always a sense of community. I often pondered how I could feel so comfortable with a room of strangers, but I realized that I was getting up to share some of my most vulnerable thoughts to these people and they were doing the same. That automatically created a closeness among everyone in attendance. The weekly routine provided relief and artistic exercise.

As a spoken word artist, I am ferocious with my delivery and healing with my truth. I take pleasure in controlling the atmosphere around me. In my life, poetry serves as my most honest form of communication. I say things in my poems that I haven't even told my closest friends. It allows me to explore my most vulnerable thoughts and feelings and make something beautiful from them. I write about any and everything of interest to me. My life, the Black experience, my Black experience, my culture, American culture, African culture, school, television, family, people, relationships, everything. I write about the random topics that I think about because I wonder if other people have thought about these topics and ideas in the same way. I write about my feelings a lot because it is not easy for me to talk to others about how I feel, so I often keep my feelings bottled up. Once it gets to the point where I can no longer hold it in, I write about it and that is how it's released. When I am writing something especially emotional, I have noticed that it is best for me to keep writing the piece until it is finished. If I try to take a break and finish it later, my mood may have changed and it then becomes difficult for me to access that raw emotion again. Once I am in that mind frame I must stay there until I have exhausted those feelings.

If I had to pick one word to sum up what spoken word is to me, it would be *therapy*.

Dream

The American Dream
A tale as old as time
White picket fences
Houses perfectly aligned
But while some elevate
Others are forced to climb
Which leaves the latter
Yearning after
The green on the other side

Susie wanna be a teacher
Johnny wanna be doctor
Reggie wanna be a rapper
Jamal wanna be a baller

Rags to riches
Road to a dollar

The
American
Dream

I wanna fly

I'm slightly battered
But it doesn't matter

Immah touch the sky

I reach to grab it
But don't feel the magic

Was it all a lie?

That was fed to me
Now it's dead to me
But I cannot cry

Wipe the water from my eyes
I've got a war to fight

Susie wanna be a teacher
Johnny wanna be doctor
Reggie wanna be a rapper
Jamal wanna be a baller

Rags to riches
Road to a dollar

THE

AMERICAN
'MERICAN
'MERICAN

Dream

5

POETRY IS MY POLITICS

Linking Spoken Word and Social Activism

Crystal Leigh Endsley

When I first began to understand that my poetry performance was connected to my politics, I was a hot mess. I had zero intention of changing anything except, maybe, the way that I felt about whatever topic I wrote about. At the time, as a budding artist who received zero mentorship as I struggled to improve, I was working through issues of identity and sexual assault. I had no clue that the stories I shared had any influence or that I had a hold of something that was central to my life's purpose. I performed because it made me feel better. Temporary relief. I was good at it, even without training. I was simply writing and performing to alleviate my own pain and hurt and because it was the only thing that gave me any clarity of thought. I was in college on a full scholarship but could not find a practical connection between the education I was receiving and my daily life. My decisions were poor, I was out of line with my own core values, and I felt lost. I used to always say, "I had no choice—the poetry chose me," but in retrospect that isn't true. I did have a choice, and every time I signed up to perform, for better or for worse, I was choosing. That choice has remained consistent for me and eventually carved out my artistry *and* sketched the blueprint of my activism.

The performance of spoken word creates a way for us to explore our own identity and how that identity impacts our relationships. Using it as pedagogy—the art of teaching and learning—the spoken word performance in a very short amount of time and with concentrated energy slices through and remixes both teaching and learning, challenging dominant power relationships and discourses. The artist and the audience have to negotiate new meanings for old concepts. And this is messy, painful work. But this rehearsal process requires that you consider your audience, your community, and your world. It is necessary because something has to change. If we want to remix the oppression, the violence, the White supremacy, the capitalism, the fear, and the doubt, then we have to change how we treat each other. We have to change how we see ourselves. Spoken word challenges, subverts, and creates new meaning for those of us who are written about, but who are rarely consulted for accuracy or effectiveness. The performance of spoken word poetry has become my politics.

The Word Made Flesh: Language and Performance

Spoken word poetry and performance have political potential as tools for social activism because of the power of language and cultural representation, and because of the direct link that poetry culture has with youth who are otherwise not engaged seriously as political actors. Because spoken word requires an audience to participate and coconstruct a performance and to negotiate the narratives being shared, the spoken word artist has the potential to motivate and initiate change within that performance space. Language is always a contested site where power dynamics are played out, and these struggles are magnified on stage during a live performance. Therefore, language, the first instrument of spoken word, has the potential to disrupt mainstream political agendas and to establish new ideologies on a larger and more accessible scale during a performance. Tremendous power is wielded through performance, and the stage easily translates as a platform for social justice.

Add to these motivating words the embodied performance that physicalizes the language and carries the *ideas* that are being shared. Spoken word performance positions the body of the student-artist (especially those from marginalized communities) as a highly contested site of political struggle as well. During a spoken word performance, student-artists are employing language and challenging the status quo, colluding with their audience, and utilizing their bodies through performance to defy and to mobilize. When student-artists enter the stage, they make use of all of the commonly represented and reproduced ideas about their bodies while simultaneously calling up their own often opposing perspectives and experiences. This challenges the audience to reconcile what they *think* they know about the body represented onstage with what that student-artist is actively telling them. What are the assumptions an audience member makes about student-artists before they even begin a poem? What are the presumed social contracts about behavior and norms before a student-artist starts a performance? The answers to these questions are where the construction of new knowledge, ideas, and solutions lie.

While centering the body is key to the power of the performance, it is also the leading risk factor for the student-artist in the uncertainty of a performance. Student-artists are fully invested, literally putting their bodies on the line to investigate the structures that shape the oppression they experience. The political spoken word performance is firmly situated within the historical, social, and political context where it takes place. For college student-artists, the content of their poetry potentially puts them at risk for speaking up and speaking out on their campus.

These insights that occur through spoken word performance create moments of transformative opportunity for us to decentralize power and to shift how we think about ourselves and one another. *What* we speak over one another and *how* we speak to one another matters.

Spoken word is such an effective tool for social change precisely because it identifies and draws attention to the embodied power relationships that it also seeks to disrupt. In my performances and in my professoring, I examine when and how such power can be mobilized toward social transformation. Performance demands that we acknowledge the body and the power that it has to shape our existence and position in society. Spoken word demands that the body of the artist be confronted; it is urgent, undeniable, and tangible. There is no abstract when it comes to embodied experience. No matter what the content of my poetry may be, you are getting that content translated through my body. Bodies determine so much of our lives, and they also determine how we perform and which of those performances elicit applause or punishment. Performance uses the body of the artist to confront audience members about their ideas around social constructs like race and gender, often at the same time. These constructs determine how we relate to each other on a daily basis. If we want to achieve social change, we must revise and rehearse our personal relationships.

Artistry and activism aren't always considered partners or even parallels. College students are positioned as consumers or customers in the neoliberal system of education, and those of us operating within such confines often struggle to put into service democratic and liberatory educational practices (Ladson-Billings, 1995; Porfilio & Yu, 2006; Richardson, 2002). What we might perceive of as hopeless and cyclical sociopolitical chaos is actually exactly the sort of environment that spoken word poetry was labored into and formed as a response. The aims and content of campus programming face new challenges that have evolved in the last decade, and yet the cultural relevancy of the open mic persists. Toby S. Jenkins's (2009) model of the roles of social change highlights three positions—ally, advocate, and agent—that provide a clear map of how to introduce, explore, and engage with social change. Spoken word poets who are also members of oppressed communities align most cogently with the role of the agent of social change, one who might be a member of a marginalized community whom Jenkins describes as "work[ing] toward creating change in the dimensions of society where they have no power" (p. 29). The student-artists who perform at campus open mic nights and use their time addressing the social issues they face are undertaking two forms of action that orient them toward social change: writing and rehearsing.

From the Page . . . Writing

Paulo Freire (1970) reminds us that "knowledge emerges only through invention and re-invention, through the restless, impatient, continuing, hopeful inquiry human beings pursue in the world, with the world and with each other" (p. 72). The performance of spoken word poetry by student-artists cultivates this rich tension of critique and reconfiguration of social injustices. If fluidity and fluency are situated as highly valued techniques and skills worth having, then the critiques produced by student-artists strive to meet those standards. Their audiences in turn develop the critical listening skills that are necessary to deconstruct and reconstruct the knowledge and assumed sociopolitical norms that are perceived as worth reproducing. Working together, student-artists and audience members can each elevate the others' practice.

The incomparable Black feminist thought theorist Patricia Hill Collins (1990) reminds us "crafting counter-hegemonic knowledge that fosters changed consciousness" (p. 285) is a top priority, especially for Black women, and thus for those of us invested in social change. Performing spoken word poetry leverages a public platform that is accessible to all students and campus constituents as a method of consciousness-changing, knowledge-producing, creative power. Through performance, spoken word poetry enables and uplifts student-artists to alter the discourse around them by going beyond what Collins (1990) calls "fending off hegemonic ideas from dominant culture" (p. 285) and instead positions student-artists as valid, worthy producers of *new* knowledge. This framework then shifts marginalized students from the defense to the offense. Student-artists are reorganized into positions of power and great social responsibility. Audience members who might not be accustomed to operating as participants in their own learning experiences are suddenly assigned an active role for each poetry performance they witness at the open mic program. The accountability the audience members experience might feel abrupt to them, particularly if their educational environment does not demand it. An implicit expectation within spoken word performances is that when the student-artist makes a call, the crowd responds. This is both a literal action and also refers to the student-artists urging social awareness, a call to action, a call to mobilize. The audience member is now a worthy producer of knowledge, expected to contribute. The ball, so to speak, is in our court, the battle is on our turf, and we make the rules. The campus open mic night functions for student-artists as a space to reset and remind themselves and their audience of the ways we can work together, within and against, to resist.

To the Stage . . . Rehearsing

How can we support our student-artists as they explore the political possibilities of their poetry? What types of leadership development programming might be needed to encourage and educate budding student-artists interested in exploring activism? How can we train student-artists for the role of civic leadership? Artists and audience members are teachers and students at the same time. As a result, for the performance of spoken word, the theory of critical pedagogy requires that we negotiate new meanings of old histories together; to be critical is to revise, continually. Artists revise our work through the process of rehearsal. We rehearse our ideas, our biases, our ways of doing things through our interactions with one another in day-to-day life. Focusing on rehearsal shifts the emphasis from the end product to the process. Rehearsal is so key to understanding who we are in relation to one another because it connects us as individual artists to the bigger picture—to our audience and the other artists with whom we share the stage. From a framework of intersectionality (see Crenshaw, 1991), rehearsal is powerful because it heightens our awareness of our own subjectivity, emphasizing our strengths and our vulnerabilities in relationship with one another. Spoken word allows us the space to be gracious during the process of rehearsal, but it demands that we commit to creating new meanings to solve old problems.

I highlight here two approaches, one individual and one group based, to expanding the role of the student-artist into that of a social activist. Open mic night plays an integral part in that it provides the space and warm invitation for student-artists to grow their artistry; however, higher stakes and broader outcomes result in growing student-artists who are now rehearsing as agents of social change.

Emerging Student-Artist Cycle

The first approach theorizes what student-artists must do on a personal level as they pursue their role as agents of social change. While that new role appears relatively simple, the burden of social responsibility is never without a cost. The role of open mic night is to provide a starting point, a meeting ground, or a fellowship where student-artists can employ, evolve, and mash up new ideas alongside the audience. The work of an emerging student-artist–activist might follow the following four steps.

Step One: Self-Reflection
The practice of writing and revising is part of critical self-reflection for any student but is especially central to the development of an emerging student-artist. So often, college students expect their first drafts of assignments to be acceptable final products and as a result turn in incomplete work that would be much improved by a second reading or draft. The same is true for spoken word poetry. Countless times I have counseled student-artists to carefully reread their work before performing it on stage because I have learned that additional readings often result in revisions that produce stronger poems. Student-artists are only as good on stage as they are on the page. Writing, while it can be guided and completed as a group, is a solitary exercise that requires discipline and commitment. This step is the most foundational of them all. Writing helps us figure out our real ideas and what we want to change. Perhaps most importantly, the more precise our writing, then the clearer our own reflection becomes.

Step Two: Connecting With the Community
To become effective at engaging an audience around a political issue, student-artists must interact with that audience. Student-artists must perform, but they must also endeavor to locate, eat, play, and ultimately dialogue with that same audience they wish to mobilize. Open mic night facilitates one aspect of connecting with the community, but the student-artist as social change agent must seek opportunities outside of programming experiences to develop real relationships with the community that is impacted by the social issues raised. Some methods include attending student organization meetings on campus, having lunch with different student groups, participating in social activities that their community hosts, and volunteering. Student-artists might explore opportunities off-campus as well.

Step Three: Negotiating Meanings
Negotiating meanings requires the student-artist to commit to the connection established in step two. It is impossible to negotiate meanings without developing a relationship that extends beyond superficial friendliness or a one-off social program. This step has no shortcut or fast track, which can be frustrating. Through solidifying dialogical relationships, student-artists learn how the community they represent on stage negotiates and navigates life *off* stage. Understanding the motivation behind daily life choices is an absolute

must in order to effect lasting social change. Student-artists must understand what justice looks like to the community they are representing, which is impossible to do without investigating the various methods of coping with, surviving, and negotiating the impossibilities, denials, and rejections that such a community employs. How does this community interact with those in power? Does it redefine words, meanings, and situations? This is often a good time for student-artists to consider their participatory role in the community. Can they sit on an advisory board? Is there a department or residence hall position that the student-artist could fill and practice the skills of negotiation? Negotiating meanings translates the lofty ambition of spoken word performance into actionable steps for student-artists in their daily campus life, requiring that a student-artist get involved. Sharing this process is a form of community building—of raising awareness to asserting simultaneously the powers of difference and collectivity.

Step Four: Reflecting on Process
Finally, the practice of reflection surfaces again, but this time with broader external considerations. What impact did connecting with the community have on the life of the student-artist and on his or her work and performance? How have those new relationships shaped the content of the poetry performed? How can student-artists practice self-care and self-affirmation in a world conspiring to silence them? At this point, the student-artist must take the time to honestly assess and consider the performance event. What was the objective? What was the impact? What was the message? What does the student-artist need to revise, rehearse, or reconsider? Again, writing should largely be the tool for this reflection.

The cycle of the emerging student-artist is not necessarily a series of graduated steps. Self-reflection often occurs throughout each step, and I often find myself swinging back and forth between two steps before I move to the next. This is not a concrete formula but rather a starting point that a student-artist might use in establishing his or her rhythm while pursuing a new avenue.

Small Group Practice for the Emerging Artist

The second approach is small group practice. Not every college cultural center or student affairs program has the capacity to support additional small-scale programming, which is understandable in the age of budget cuts and political setbacks for all diversity and multicultural initiatives. However, this approach is one of the most effective ways to support student-artists who are exploring their political voices as it demonstrates collective and participatory action as well as collaboration. There is no such thing as too much emphasis on the message that is sent when institutional programming responds effectively to students' needs; such response is a direct and clear action that demonstrates a value for the holistic well-being of the students. When those students are underrepresented, marginalized, and the targets of racism, sexism, and classism, the institution is even more accountable for providing structural support.

Small group practice for the emerging artist provides development for student-artists in a group setting. The structure of a small group practice for the emerging artist is organized to follow the cycle of the emerging student-artist, and the workshops or sessions should be framed accordingly. An explanation of each step follows.

Step One: Reflexive Group Writing

Each small group meeting should begin with a writing exercise. There are benefits associated with any writing produced during the creative process; however, I have found that if student-artists learn to expect to begin each workshop with a writing prompt, it provides focus and centers them to be present in the workshop space with less external distraction. Our students' lives are already crammed to the brim with business, and it is important to distinguish this time as separate, selective, and a blank slate.

Step Two: Link Up

In correspondence with step two of the cycles of the emerging student-artist, the small group should spend some time exploring each student's community memberships. Where do they feel a commitment and why? What is their motivation for participating with those communities? How might students connect with the communities? A large part of the initial meetings will be to create opportunities for the student-artists to explore their own identities and how those identities play a part in their politics. Provide the time, resources, and guidance for the student-artists to research the communities they most want to connect with and then facilitate those networks. The student-artists will bring their own ideas and desires for artistic growth to the table. As the facilitator of a small group, the impetus for skill-building is part of your job. Figure out where the student-artists might perform that will challenge them with a new audience and a new environment off campus.

Step Three: Key Players

Once the student-artists begin making connections with their community, guide them in recognizing key players on campus and in their communities. One gateway approach to involving someone new is inviting a guest artist to visit a small group meeting. Introducing new styles, artists, practices, and methods for approaching spoken word performance is critical to a lasting artistic journey. Is there a guest speaker coming to campus who might be willing to lead a writing workshop with the student-artists? This activity would expand the student-artists' view as they continue to work on their craft. As they become more informed citizens, their artistic practice will improve. Perhaps the student-artists might want to identify and invite a few key players from a particular demographic on campus to one of their small group meetings in order to have an intimate dialogue about how that key player became politically involved. Key players aren't all artists, and sometimes they are not even students. Consider administration members who might provide insight to a historical institutional struggle. Perhaps the director of the campus art museum might offer some tips on handling the business or logistical side of the arts. This is a chance to introduce the student-artists to key players and also to showcase the work that student-artists have been writing and performing.

Step Four: Re-Vision

Think about the word *revision*. This term can be defined in two ways. We typically think about revising in terms of rewriting a draft of a poem, for example. However, in this step of the small group meetings, *re-vision* means reflecting on the two visions that should have surfaced for the student–artists. The first vision consists of the students' own personal goals as artists. What do they want? Where do they want to go? What are their challenges, and how do they want to address them? The second vision is for the community of the small group of emerging artists as a whole. Revisit the initial objectives you might have designed when the program began, and remind the group of those goals. Ask the small group if those goals have been achieved, and address why or why not.

Most important, do not neglect your own reflection process in this step. Do any aspects of the vision need to be rewritten? As a small group, the emerging student-artists will have reached a point that they are ready to assess and reflect collectively. The practice of collective reflection is difficult because there are always competing desires in any small group. If you enter this step understanding that there will likely be resistance or even a need to examine your own goals, then you are halfway there. The re-visioning might consume multiple meetings and may take on different formats. Find what works for your small group's dynamic, and they will have gained another technique for their own artistry and activism.

Like most programming, small group practice for the emerging artist will likely take on a collaborative format that invites buy-in and support from multiple offices on campus. Consider pairing up with a student worker or assistant who might be interested or have experience in shaping a curriculum for an arts-as-activism course or workshop series. Feel free to scale the intensity of these steps to match your small group of emerging artists as they enter the process of coming to terms with their role as social change agents at various levels. Consistency is the most crucial factor when beginning a small group, and sustaining the consistency—of meetings, of expectations, of writing assignments—will likely meet with refusal from some student-artists initially. This is not an indication of a group's success or failure. Consistency shapes the student-artists' ability to face struggle outside of their small group meetings, and they will have a reference point for how to cope when they come up against obstacles.

Conclusion

The performance of spoken word poetry creates the space for us to examine outside of ourselves our relationships and imagine how we might relate to one another differently. The moments of performance are also the moments of social transformation because we take those new ideas, cocreated by the artist and the audience, and then rehearse the possibilities we imagine together in our everyday lives and social interactions. That is how spoken word creates social justice.

So we must teach and learn—we must revise and rehearse, we must forgive and then become vulnerable. The cycle of the emerging student-artist provides a frame of reference for understanding how a new poet becomes politically engaged. The small group meetings for emerging student-artists outline an organizational framework that provides a structure for support of those new poets who need nurturing and guidance in their quest for social justice. Spoken word poetry performance opens up room for student-artists and audience members to explore growing politically, and consistent open mic programs and additional smaller-scale practices supply good ground, regular watering, and hopefully the chance to reap a harvest (Gomez-Pena & Sifuentes, 2011). Together, artist and audience imagine new possibilities for resistance and new social change strategies. The reality is that we must combine the spirit with the physical, the visceral with the intangible, in order to change. We must rehearse—again and again and again—until we get it right.

References

Collins, P. H. (1990). *Black feminist thought: Knowledge, consciousness, and the politics of empowerment*. 2nd ed. New York, NY: Routledge.

Crenshaw, K. (1991). Mapping the margins: Intersectionality, identity politics, and violence against women of color. *Stanford Law Review, 43*(6), 1241–1299.

Freire, P. (1970). *Pedagogy of the oppressed*. New York, NY: Continuum.

Gomez-Pena, G., & Sifuentes, R. (2011). *Exercises for the rebel artist: Radical performance pedagogy*. New York, NY: Routledge.

Jenkins, T. S. (2009). Bottom line: A seat at the table that I set: Beyond social justice allies. *About Campus, 14*(5), 27–29.

Ladson-Billings, G. (1995). But that's just good teaching: The case for culturally relevant pedagogy. *Theory Into Practice, 34*(3), 159–165.

Porfilio, B., and Yu, T. (2006). "Student as consumer": A critical narrative of the commercialization of teacher education. *Journal for Critical Education Policy Studies, 4*(1), 1–14.

Richardson, E. (2002). *African American literacies*. New York, NY: Routledge.

Student Voices

Terri Moise

Student, Hamilton College

Poet Self-Portrait

For the past few years of my life, I have been searching for something. I did not know how to explain what I was looking for; I just knew that when I found it, I would feel it in my heart. It was not until I returned home for winter break after my first semester of college that I finally found that feeling. All that time, I had been searching for home. For me, *home* was a complex and foreign concept. I knew that when I was with my family I was home, but I questioned whether that was the only time that was possible. How do I feel comfortable in spaces not my own? How do I embrace those around me when they are not family? How do I reach out to those around me and let them hear my voice?

When I wrote my first poem, I was trying to figure out how to say the things I could not say out loud. When I performed my first spoken word piece, I was trying to build up the courage to use my voice to speak my truth. And when I stood on my first stage, I was trying to speak the words I felt the world needed to hear.

Poetry and spoken word are both unique ways in which we can reach people. I believe these forms of expression serve as bridge builders, connecting not only the minds but also the hearts of individuals. Sometimes when I read poetry, I feel as if the poet's words are an invitation to sit with her or him and talk about anything in the world. When I hear a spoken word piece being performed, I feel as if I can hear the sorrows, joys, and all the things in between in the performer's voice, as if the performer's words are merely a vehicle with which to bring the audience that much closer to understanding the performer as well as themselves. These things have helped me realize that poetry and spoken word have helped me to find a voice and to use that voice to build a community.

For me, poetry and spoken word have served multiple roles in my life. During my time in college, I have been involved with the Feminists of Color Collective (FCC), an organization focused on unpacking and understanding the ways in which art can be political, using poetry, painting, and song to talk about issues of race, gender, and sexuality. Every semester, FCC puts on SpeakEasy, an open mic and poetry lounge where students come and perform pieces close to their heart. When I went to my first SpeakEasy, I was astounded at the talent and power within the performers; however, what really surprised me was how connected to the performers I felt and how inspired I felt to perform my own piece, stage fright be damned. I promised to myself that one day I would be out there performing and sharing myself.

The following semester, I made good on that promise. Earlier that semester, a peer had sexually assaulted me. I did not know how to talk about it without breaking down, for my mouth felt heavy every time I tried to let out that truth. Bit by bit, holding that truth inside was killing me, as my assaulter was still on campus and now assaulting other individuals. One day, as I was twirling a pen in my hand, I wrote the first words of a piece I titled "The Demon's Grasp." As I worked on this piece, another peer of mine confided in me that the same individual had assaulted them as well. Angry, hurt, and looking to be free of the pain, we worked on the piece together and performed it at the next SpeakEasy.

Standing on that stage with my friend, with the words flowing from our mouths as if they were streams of water from a fountain, I felt powerful, significant, and strong. After the performance, the audience clapped for a few minutes, with many audience members giving a standing ovation. Looking around the room, I felt as if my voice had been finally heard and would no longer fall on deaf ears. One member of the audience came up to my friend and me and told us that, after the piece we performed, he felt as if he understood the two of us a bit better.

With the help of poetry and spoken word, it felt like I had finally found somewhere else that I could call home. For the next few semesters, SpeakEasy continued to happen, and each time I felt my bond with the other performers and the audience growing stronger. This past SpeakEasy especially demonstrated to me that these bonds had only strengthened over time. As I cohosted the event, all I saw were joy, community, and strength. With every poem performed and every song sung, it felt like the community was becoming stronger. Even in a place where I had been hurt, I had found a haven, a place where I could lay my pen to rest and let my voice ring out instead.

I had found a place where I could finally say, "This is where I am home."

Where I Am Home

I am home in the pages of novels and stories,
Each page carrying me deeper and deeper
Into realms unknown, seas uncharted, worlds unexplored.
Each character speaking to me,
Conversing with me in foreign tongues,
Yet sounding like the lullabies of my youth.

Each villain, and each hero, pushing my boundaries,
The boundaries of my thoughts,
For now my imagination has become limitless, eternally
Infinite.

I am home in the words of poetry,
The metaphors and similes not only transforming the words,
But transforming my soul, leading me into a new place,
A place of wonder and power,
In which my pen is not only my sword, but my shield,
Where the words leap and dance,
Where allusions and hyperbole live just over yonder.
The poems of the greats feeding my mind,
I live in a home made of such
Beauty.

I am home in my mother's arms,
I am home in my sisters' laughs,
I am home in my brothers' smiles,
For they breathe life into me,
They are my essence, my soul, my power,
For before I branched out,
They were my roots,
Before I could fly,
They became my wings, wings of such
Magnificence.

Where am I home?
I am home in the worlds of myths and stories,
In a place where I am
Infinite.

Where am I home?
I am home in the songs of the hearts,
Where the mouth moves little, yet the soul speaks volumes,
In a place of unimaginable
Beauty.

Where am I home?
I am home in the hearts of my sisters,
I am home in the dances of my brothers,

I am home in the soul of my mother,
I am home in a family of pure and utter
Magnificence.

Where am I home?
I am home with
You.

6

SOCIAL JUSTICE EDUCATION AIN'T PRETTY

A Case for Hip-Hop Feminist Studies

Marla L. Jaksch

I reflected and discovered things about myself that I had never known before. I experienced the power of spoken word and gained an understanding of how it can be used for social justice.

—Olivia (student, personal communication, October 2016)

This chapter explores the challenges, as well as the promise, that come with engaging students in exploring intersecting concepts like race, class, gender, sexuality, and (dis)ability in social justice education—especially when those approaches are intersectional in nature. Intersectional ways of thinking are foundational to social justice education because, as an analytical tool, intersectional thinking has the capacity to assist us in solving problems and achieving educational equity. While intersectionality consists of incredibly heterogeneous approaches, Collins and Bilge (2016) contend,

> Intersectionality is a way of understanding and analyzing the complexity of the world, in people, and in human experiences. The events and conditions of social and political life and the self can seldom be understood as shaped by one factor. They are generally shaped by many factors in diverse and mutually influencing ways. When it comes to social inequality, people's lives and the organization of power in a given society are better understood as being shaped not by a single axis of social division, be it race or gender or class, but by many axes that work together and influence each other. Intersectionality as an analytic tool gives people better access to the complexity of the world and themselves. (p. 2)

Schools are more than just locations where students go to learn the skills necessary to get a good job (although within neoliberal frameworks of education, more and more colleges do market themselves this way). Schools are also "venues where intersecting power relations of race, class, gender, sexuality, nationality, ethnicity, ability and age routinely privilege some students over others" (Collins & Bilge, 2016, p. 165). In order to challenge this inequality and to better prepare students with the ability to navigate higher education and beyond, we need to diversify our theories and practices. Hip-hop feminist studies provide us with useful ways of thinking about the application of intersectionality and inclusivity as praxis. According to Zenele Isoke (2010), hip-hop feminism

> effectively challenges and transforms power structures, social order, and widespread cultural practices, and [proves] to be [an] efficacious intersectional strategy for understanding complex identities and difference in Women's Studies and across academic disciplines. Simultaneously, hip-hop feminism engages effective grassroots community-based social justice movements across transnational frameworks. (Quoted in Durham, 2010, p. 134n1)

Hip-hop feminists have developed theories and practices that have significant transformational potential (Brown, 2008, 2013; Brown & Kwakye, 2012), but these approaches "remain relatively underutilized and unrecognized as liberatory and resistive strategies for social justice in and beyond education" (Lindsey, 2015, p. 54). Given the potential that higher education can play in addressing inequality, compounded by demographic shifts that continue to transform higher education, I argue for the incorporation of intersectional hip-hop feminist studies, which includes spoken word, as an important social justice theory and praxis in student affairs.

The Open in Open Mic on Campus: Toward an Inclusive Community

> The idea that spoken word, hip-hop, and the arts in general do not have to be separate from the academic world is not a common belief. (Katrina, student, personal communication, October 2016)

On May 5, 2016, spoken word took center stage at Harvard's Graduate School of Education's graduation ceremony when master's student Donovan Livingston gave the convocation address. Although not the traditional open mic setting, Livingston performed a poem about the politics of education—specifically the barriers that Black and Brown youth must overcome in educational settings. His performance speaks to the utility of spoken word in creating a space for our students to experience inclusion and affirmation within institutional spaces. In the introduction to his May 2016 spoken word address, Livingston shared,

> When I spoke at my high school graduation several years ago, my high school English teacher threatened to replace me on the program or cut the microphone when she found out that I was interested in doing a poem as a part of my remarks, um, so I am eternally grateful for being able to share this piece of myself in my most authentic voice with you this afternoon. So, spoken word poetry insists on participation, so if you feel so compelled— snap, clap, throw up your hands, rejoice, and celebrate. (Livingston, 2016)

The more than 2,200 people in attendance participated by doing just that. In audio and video recordings of the address you can hear the crowd speak back, clap, stomp, and whoop and cheer him on. Video of Livingston's spoken word address went viral, and within hours of the address being posted, the video received more than five million views. While one interpretation of the popularity of this performance might be due to its entertainment value, I would argue for additional interpretations.

In mapping an alternative genealogy of hip-hop feminist media studies, Alisha Durham (2010) offers many exercises and examples of decoding hiphop visual culture. For example, Durham (2010) argues that through a hip-hop feminist studies, the "interpretive possibilities are abundant, especially when we represent embodied knowledge in forms devalued in the academy (e.g., spoken word)" (p. 130). Livingston (2016), through his spoken word address and corresponding video, invites the public sphere to see spoken word and education through the lens of a young man of color and redefines the spoken word cipher as something that happens only outside of academia.

Hip-hop and spoken word poetry center the storytelling, authentic voice, story exchange, and naming of one's own reality especially as these expressions intersect with race, class, and gender consciousness with the goal of social change and transformation (Delgado, 1990). Spoken word constitutes a vitally important site where the narratives of young people reflect the complexity of their lived experience. Typically, in spaces where spoken word is performed, artists share incredibly personal perspectives that might touch on issues from rape culture and sexual assault to being so poor that their utilities are shut off, to being kicked out of the house because of their sexual identity, to experiencing violence in their home or their community, to the dreadful conditions of their schools. They do this publicly, often to a supportive community that they work to create and maintain. In describing the function of Bed, The Pennsylvania State University's Park campus open mic program that she cofounded, Crystal Leigh Endsley (2016) highlights the need for creative, productive outlets for students, many of whom transitioned from major urban centers to a rural locations with few people of color. Endsley (2016) states,

> The open mic represented to these student artists an opportunity to voice their discontent with their current surroundings and environment, a chance to declare how they see themselves and their roles despite images portrayed by history books or popular culture. The opportunity for creative expression surrounding social justice issues is also particularly salient as there is a tense history of racial conflict on our campus. (p. 60)

In this way, spoken word becomes a site of healing from the injuries of different types of oppression and "demonstrate[s] the significance of art as a place of love, healing, and intimacy" (Collins & Bilge, 2016, p. 121). Programs such as Bed, the spoken word program started by Toby S. Jenkins with the support of Crystal Leigh Endsley and Anthony Keith Jr. at The Pennsylvania State University, recognize college campuses as politically, socially, and culturally complicated sites with histories of creating and maintaining inequalities. In fact, many campuses spend a great deal of time and effort forgetting these troubling histories.

Livingston's (2016) spoken word address makes visible tensions that emerge when we break from the status quo—whether in who does the speaking; where and in what style, format, or language; and what topics are tackled. Hip-hop can be seen as an important form of cultural politics because it focuses on the variety of problems young people face day to day and serves as a space for political expression (Clay, 2012). The practices associated with hip-hop—for example, poetry that criticizes schools and the police, tagging public spaces, and refusing to follow or questioning the rules—disrupt the status quo. In his poem, Livingston (2016) specifically addresses the politics of race and higher education, and speaks truth to power when he spits,

> Unfortunately, I've seen more dividing and conquering
> In this order of operations—a heinous miscalculation of reality.
> For some, the only difference between a classroom and a plantation is time.
> How many times must we be made to feel like quotas—
> Like tokens in coined phrases?—
> "Diversity. Inclusion."
> There are days I feel like one, like only—
> A lonely blossom in a briar patch of broken promises.
> But I've always been a thorn in the side of injustice.

Here, Livingston makes visible and palpable how the process of schooling has felt for him, and while doing so he confronts the institution that has shaped him so profoundly. Youth typically spend more time in educational spaces than all others, and as a result, school can be an important location for activism. Collins and Bilge (2016) propose that when "college students develop a critical consciousness about social inequality, their examples are drawn from their school experiences because that's where they spend their time" (p. 167). In this way, spoken word provides a space to talk about the quality of and dissatisfaction with schooling, and it becomes a way to talk to others who have a shared experience, as well as to educate those who have historically benefitted from the status quo within education systems and programs. Moreover, by taking seriously young people's perspectives, we acknowledge that age is a significant intersectional identity and a category that cuts across other categories. For example, young people experience inequalities that are related to age as a system of power. As such, young people have

> a special vantage point in the intersection of social inequalities of ethnicity, religion, gender, sexuality, and race. They know that their neighborhoods receive inferior services and special policing. They see how their schools have less experienced teachers, old and dilapidated buildings, and outdated textbooks. They know that jobs for teenagers are minimal, and that the legitimate jobs that do exist pay little and have few benefits. Race, class, gender, and citizenship categories disadvantage many groups under neoliberal policies, yet, because age straddles all of these categories, young people's experiences of social problems are more intensified. (Collins & Bilge, 2016, p. 117)

Livingston's (2016) address and his invitation to join in (and therefore be a part of community via spoken word performance) reveals how collaborative performance is a powerful strategy in advocating for change. Durham (2010) explains, "Exploiting the emotive and evocative power of language, performance compels us to (re)act at a visceral level. Performance privileges embodied ways of knowing" (p. 129). The *open* part of open mic is an invitation to speak freely. And it may very well be a clap back. It's meant to be dialogic. What did Livingston's high school teacher fear in his performance of a poem? What might it reveal regarding the pressure students face in assimilating and conforming, about keeping silent or not being able to ask or answer a question not posed by the teacher?

Building a diverse and inclusive campus community is a stated common goal among institutions of higher education. And if we take seriously Livingston's critiques of what it feels like to be at an institution of higher education—but not a part of it—we are compelled to listen and respond by expanding the approaches to reaching these goals.

How many times must we be made to feel like quotas—
Like tokens in coined phrases?—
"Diversity. Inclusion."
There are days I feel like one, like only—
A lonely blossom in a briar patch of broken promises. (Livingston, 2016)

Especially given how evident social divisions on campus are and will likely continue to be, should we choose to move ahead with the current approaches? The racial, ethnic, and socioeconomic makeup of students entering higher education is rapidly shifting. By 2020, 45% of the nation's public high school graduates will be non-White, compared to 38% in 2009. These students will more likely be the first in their family to attend college and have less economic means. In addition to more adult learners joining the ranks of higher education, there will also be an increase of foreign-born immigrants and international students specifically recruited by colleges.

In an effort to create more inclusive campus environments for current students and to make progress to accommodate the demographic shifts under way, colleges have adopted more explicit values and practices that attempt to achieve these goals, as Livingston's address (2016) confirms. It is becoming more common that student affairs offices find themselves at the center of this effort—with access to spaces, funding for events, full- and part-time administrative staff, and dedicated time. But the focus on inclusion in the cocurricular environment has also been driven by an understanding that inclusion is not just an intellectual enterprise. Out-of-classroom environments are ripe with opportunities for students to process, communicate, and engage around the topics and intersections of racial, gender, and class identities; sexual diversity; and disabilities. As a result, student affairs professionals are often expected to support students in those settings.

A recent survey by the American Council on Higher Education found that a "majority of college presidents rely on their student affairs professionals to address racial issues. Such roles have often resulted in student affairs professionals serving as a type of first respondent to campus developments" (Espinosa, Chessman, & Wayt, 2016). It is also worth noting that a majority of presidents commented that they heavily rely upon nonsenior student affairs staff (as well as campus-wide diversity committees and legal counsel) in addressing diversity and inclusivity-related issues. Sara Ahmed (2012) explores the gap between symbolic commitments to diversity and the experience of those who embody diversity, as well as the challenges in defining and doing diversity work. Her findings suggest that we need to be critical of a simplistic understanding of diversity. While the "demographic imperative" (Parnell, 2016) may be driving changes in higher education, Collins and Bilge (2016) caution against an approach that locates the need for diversity training in a presumed "mismatch" between young people who will likely attend college (and K–12 schools) and a professional staff that remains overwhelmingly White as "misdiagnoses of the problem" (p. 174). Rather, they argue that diversity initiatives "that work with the complex identities that are important to students and that see these identities as linked to broader structural forces retain ties to multiculturalism and intersectionality" (p. 175). In doing so, we move beyond merely helping students better fit into existing systems that may not be safe or equitable, and we begin to see the ways that different praxes assist us in transforming the institution by validating students as knowers.

As I suggested at the beginning of this chapter, hip-hop feminist studies practitioners have taken up these questions. The various hip-hop feminist theories and praxes devised provide us with some compelling ways to integrate these theories and praxes into our work inside and outside the classroom. They bring us full circle to the conversations shared at the very beginning of this book. Hip-hop feminist theory provides us with important strategies to confront the challenges that Robb Ryan Q. Thibault, the author of this book's introduction, poses as important to student affairs professionals: how to create spaces where freedom of speech and inclusivity coexist and how to facilitate important "ouch" moments for our students. In the following section, I provide an overview of feminist hip-hop studies and conclude with examples of hip-hop feminist pedagogy in action.

Hip-Hop Feminist Theory and Pedagogy: It May Not Be Pretty, but It Sho' Can Be Transformative

> Then it all of a sudden made sense to me. If students are able to use spoken word poetry, pull from personal experiences, and use their artistic interpretations in the classroom, amazing things can happen. (Elizabeth, student journal, 2016)

> Art embodies social change and alters perceptions of the world. When people can represent themselves through art, they invite others to make connections and grasp a deeper meaning of their identities. (Erika, student journal, 2016)

For more than 40 years, girls and women have played substantial and varied roles in *hip-hop*, predating the term itself. This engagement goes well beyond the formation and support of hip-hop culture. Rather, girls' and women's engagements with hip-hop "provide distinct stand-points, perspectives, and interventions" (Lindsey, 2015, p. 53). Despite the large and growing body of work that resolutely affirms the impor-tance of women and girls in hip-hop transnationally, there continues to be a devaluation of women's and girls' significance in and to hip-hop and beyond (Brown, 2008; Brown & Kwakye, 2012; Durham, Cooper, & Morris, 2013; Endsley, 2016; Gaunt, 2006; Lindsey, 2015; Love, 2012; Morgan, 1999; Pough, 2003; Pough, Richardson, Durham, & Raimist, 2007; Rivera, 2003; Sharpley-Whiting, 2008). Treva Lindsey (2015) argues that this continued devaluation "remains a primary concern for sustaining progressive, anti-sexist, and anti-misogynistic gender and sexual politics within hip-hop" and beyond, because this devaluation can "contribute to the marginalization of girls in classrooms and community-based education initiatives and programs" (p. 53).

Aisha Durham, Brittney C. Cooper, and Susana M. Morris (2013) map the rich and varied past, present, and future of hip-hop feminist studies by considering the dialogic relationship between feminism and hip-hop that meets to create a critical hip-hop feminism. They write, "The creative, intel-lectual work of hip-hop feminism invites new questions about representa-tion, provides additional insights about embodied experience, and offers alternative models for critical engagement" (p. 722). The authors map the emergence of the field of hip-hop feminism through the groundbreaking work of Joan Morgan (1999; 2006) and Gwendolyn D. Pough (2003) that created a space for hip-hop feminists with an insistence on "living with con-tradiction, because failure to do so relegates feminism to an academic project that is not politically sustainable beyond the ivory tower" (Durham et al., 2013, p. 723).

Lindsey (2015) makes a compelling argument for the incorporation of hip-hop feminist theory in social justice education generally by suggesting,

> Hip-hop feminist theory is not a new direction in hip-hop feminism per se, but recognizing and engaging the theoretical labor of hip-hop feminists. . . . The fuller incorporation of hip-hop feminist theory could assist those working in [urban] education settings by being more inclusive of the expe-riences, perspectives, and standpoints of Black and Brown and girls and young women. (p. 54)

In making the case for the utility of hip-hop feminist theoretical inter-ventions, Lindsey (2015) highlights a few of the most prominent approaches, which include "bringing wreck, kinetic orality, sonic pleasure, percussive resistance, and Black girl standpoint theory" (p. 55). These theoretical interventions make visible the work that girls and women do, whether in challenging sexism, misogynoir, rape culture in hip-hop culture and community, or the devaluation of women's and girls' artistic and cultural practices.

The publishing of Joan Morgan's book (1999) stands as a transformative moment, in part because Morgan coins the term *hip-hop feminist*, but also because she articulates a feminist theory and a vision of "a feminism brave enough to 'fuck with the grays'" (p. 59). *Fuckin' with the grays* provides a way to understand the multiple social locations that women and girls occupy and renders visible the tensions and contradictions present between people's lived experiences and their political standpoints. When hip-hop feminists "refuse easy and essentialist political stances about what is right or wrong and who or what gets to be called feminist," they create a space for building—not just critique or deconstruction (Durham et al., 2013, p. 723). Hip-hop feminism as a space of building led Gwendolyn D. Pough (2003) to introduce the concept of hip-hop pedagogy as a foundational praxis of hip-hop feminist studies. Ruth Nicole Brown and Chamara Jewel Kwakye (2012) describe hip-hop feminist pedagogy as one that

> 1) appreciates creative production expressed through language, art, or activism; 2) privileges the in-betweenness of a black girl epistemology or a black feminist standpoint; 3) values and cares about the shared knowledge produced by black women's and girls' presence; 4) interrogates the limitations and possibilities of Hip-hop, feminism, and pedagogy and is, therefore, self-adjusting; 5) stages the political through performance-based cultural criticism; 6) is located and interpreted through the community (or communities) in which it is immersed. (p. 4)

The approach that Brown and Kwakye (2012) outline is useful in creating a space within classrooms or other educational spaces for inclusivity and transformation—of individuals, communities, and institutions.

In the fall of 2016 I offered a Gender Equity in Education course at The College of New Jersey (TCNJ). The students in the course consisted of mostly urban education majors, but the course was offered through the Women's, Gender, and Sexuality Studies Department. In this course, I introduced hip-hop feminist studies as a key theoretical framework for the course and employed pedagogical strategies like the ones that Brown and Kwakye (2012) describe. In response to a spoken word and social justice workshop offered as a part of the course, a student reflected, "It was after this performance that I realized the significance between drawing an emotional connection between my future students, and myself, whether that is through spoken word or other art mediums. Analouise Keating touches upon how we are all interconnected and that interconnectedness is what 'can empower us to change' (Keating, 2007, p. 29)" (Jessica [pseudonym], personal communication, 2016). Expression through art is a way to promote and facilitate connections, understandings, and appreciations for one another. Although connections might not be evident through physical identities, there are ways to form connections through aspects of internal identities. This was one of the most influential workshops I have ever experienced for both my future teaching career and personal self because the reflections brought to life the value and meaning behind knowing myself, building a classroom community, and steps I can take to effectively bridge them together. Another student reflected,

> The idea that everyone embodies many different identities that overlap and conflict at the same time helps us better understand ourselves and our students. Although we may feel like we are, no one is alone in this trait of humanity. No one is one-dimensional or simplistic. Stereotypes cloud our perspectives about each other and diminish our individuality. It is important that we truly attempt to build strong relationships with one another if we ever want to see real social change. (from a student journal)

Keating (2007) emphasizes the need to forge "new" stories. She argues that the deeply engrained status quo stories that center meritocracy and suggest we all have access to equal opportunities and fair treatment need to be reworked. Keating (2007) emphasizes the ability of a powerful story to change the world. She argues, "We need different stories about reality, stories that enable us to question the status quo and transform our existing situations" (p. 29).

The student's journal quote articulates one of the goals of hip-hop feminist pedagogy: to provide new, creative ways to teach and develop the skills necessary to build a more inclusive community. By facilitating workshops in which spoken word artists join the classroom to discuss their work, we expose students to "independent art in order to raise awareness about alternative spaces of cultural production" (Gwendolyn, Richardson, Durham, & Raimist, 2007, p. 126), and in doing so we provide alternative ways to knowing and being in the world.

Devising pedagogical strategies that challenge students' perceptions allows for a reorganization and redefinition of individual and communal identities that challenge the status quo. One of my students reflected that he experienced the performance of spoken word in our class in a visceral, embodied way. He shared, "Her life experience poured out through the words she chose to use. Her body language and passion felt like it went beyond the walls of our classroom. I have heard spoken word poetry before but never like that."

Language itself is a material reality that can connect us as a community. However, the words we use come to us already steeped with meaning and importance. As such, we are connected linguistically, but we can remix these connections. For example, Keating (2007) suggests that by "locating each individual within a larger, holistic context . . . human beings are not self-enclosed. We are indeed distinct entities, we also share permeable boundaries" (p. 31). Moreover, as Gloria Anzaldua (2000) explains, "The self can penetrate other things and they penetrate you" (p. 162). Building on Anzaldua's (2000) understanding of permeability, Keating (2007) adapts this view to consider the ways this view situates relational forms of identity that value both "personal and collective integrity and self-respect" (p. 31) over more solipsistic ones. This understanding of the permeability of selves imagines that we

> extend outward . . . meeting, touching, entering into exchange with other subjects (human and nonhuman alike). Significantly, this outward movement is not an imperialistic appropriation where an egocentric subject grows larger by extending its boundaries to incorporate or annihilate every object in its path. It is, rather, a mutual encounter between subjects. This definition invites students to shift perspectives and adopt a much broader—though inevitably partial—point of view. (Keating, 2007, p. 31)

Keating's (2007) understanding of permeability allows us to comprehend how my student experienced the spoken word as an embodiment of social justice pedagogy (Endsley, 2016). As the spoken word artist performed, he physically felt connected in a way that challenged his past experiences both with spoken word and with learning in a classroom setting. He was not the only student who reflected upon this aspect. Another student commented,

> While her rhymes and use of metaphors were incredible, the way that she delivered those words was everything. You felt her passion and pain, and took part in a shared visceral experience. That is the power of spoken word. You can walk into a performance without knowing anything about a person, but leave feeling like you have lived their entire life in their body. You have no choice but to meet them on their "emotional turf," as Emdin would say, and I think this is how we change hearts and minds. Lived experience is one of the most powerful things, and creating spaces for people to hear the stories and struggles of those who are different from them is what I think will be those "millimeters" that lead to big changes.

This student's description further elucidates what Keating (2007) describes as an ethics of openness, reciprocity, and exchange. I find deep synergies between Keating's work and those in hip-hop feminist studies that demand approaches to teaching that are grounded in the lived experiences of the marginalized, specifically the lives of girls and women of color, and are approached from nonessentialized understandings of identities—and yet have the political potential to forge commonalities and connection within and across difference.

As hip-hop education scholar Christopher Emdin (2016) writes, "Students quickly receive the message that they can only be smart when they are not who they are" (p. 27). To address this issue, Emdin (2016) argues that teachers must use culturally relevant pedagogy, a method that "advocates for a consideration of the culture of the students in determining the ways in which they are taught" (p. 27). Tools of the open mic—which include monologues, poetry, storytelling of many styles and types, and musical performance—can be useful in achieving a culturally relevant pedagogy. In her reflection about our workshop, another student wrote about seeing the worlds of academia and spoken word collide.

> As I said before, these are two big passions of mine, but I have always seen them as mutually exclusive. I have never considered how they can be used in collaboration to explore areas that each entity on its own cannot represent fully. I also really appreciated hearing about pioneering work to build bridges across different worlds, which has challenged me to reflect more seriously on my passions and interests, and to think about ways to reimagine what can be done in a classroom setting or investigated in a research question.

For my student, teaching meant adopting another identity, minimizing her own, and ignoring the culture and knowledge that students bring to the classroom in lieu of more respectable approaches. It was revelatory for this student to be given the permission or the space to consider the two together. An ethics of openness, reciprocity, and exchange also creates a space for conflict. The exchange and openness cannot be passive. In the final student reflection I share, the student notes that each of us brings complicated, unexamined, and unacknowledged stuff—"baggage"—to the classroom, and this baggage includes our multiple identities. My student reflects upon "how important it is to recognize and work with all of the baggage each individual student brings to the classroom" (Emdin, 2016, p. 43). In a classroom community, every individual has something of value to contribute regardless of or because of his or her baggage. In order to foster this community, teachers need to start by being aware and recognizing their own identities and how those identities influence their pedagogy and perspectives. Teachers must strive to create an environment where their own identities can blend with the identities of each individual student. The exchange that occurs between identities from teacher to student and from student to student should be mutual, and all parties involved should be held accountable. The ideas of belonging and exchange are essential to community. They build the culture, and culture is the glue that keeps a community together.

Our identities and realities are shaped by a cluster of beliefs, perceptions, language, culture, and actions, and they in turn shape how we come to understand ourselves. This cluster also includes the media, our education, family, and community. Stuart Hall (1990) argues, "How we 'see' ourselves and our social relations matters, because it enters into and informs our actions and practices" (p. 272). When we create alternative spaces to see ourselves and others, we begin to do the work of change, which can lead to social change and justice.

As I have argued throughout this chapter, hip-hop feminist studies, which includes hip-hop feminist pedagogies, provides the required tools, frameworks, and paradigms for strengthening our approaches to educating for social justice inside or outside the classroom (Lindsey, 2015). But we must democratize this work. Assuming that only African Americans will be interested in hip-hop, or only women will be interested in women's and gender studies, or only LGBTQ students will be interested in queer studies merely reifies the silo approach to programming that currently exists on many campuses. In 2016, a TCNJ student, tired of the lack of programming that addressed overlaps in identity, designed an Intersectionality Week that included intersectionality monologues. This is an important step toward reimagining and building an inclusive campus. Hip-hop feminism reminds us that "inclusivity should be at the core of both hip-hop and social justice based education" (Lindsey, 2015, p. 74). Given the stated desire of college campuses to be more inclusive, adopting hip-hop feminist studies praxis provides a variety of tools for decentering and strengthening social justice–based education in higher education.

Conclusion

In this chapter, my goal was to offer the perspective of educators and scholar-practitioners. This perspective allows us to understand more critically what spoken word is as a political, personal, cultural, and developmental space for college students, as well as its position as a transformative education space for all who experience it—community members, artists, teachers, and practitioners. This art form is part of a larger culture, which makes the students who participate in it part of a larger community, which is also why the authors of this book have centered the chapters not only in the scholarship and literature but also in our own experiences as scholars, student affairs practitioners, teachers, and people.

We also offer perspective in the form of strategies to create successful and intentional programming. In creating open mic spaces, we are delving into complicated and sensitive territory. We are creating spaces for students to share raw opinions and personal experiences and to unpack the baggage that they bring from their very complicated lives. Words in these spaces might make you laugh or cry; they might make you think and reconsider; and they might push, challenge, or sometimes even hurt. Facilitating these programs requires a more critical and intentional approach than simply booking a room, building a stage, and setting a mic in the center. This is why we share the theoretical concept of hip-hop feminism, which can be integrated into student affairs professional practice. Building educational experiences from an informed perspective that includes the principles of hip-hop feminist theory, the strategies of intentional programming, and the authentic appreciation of the art and culture of spoken word can help us to create truly transformative educational experiences.

References

Ahmed, S. (2012). *On being included: Racism and diversity in institutional life.* Durham, NC: Duke University Press.

Anzaldua, G. (2000). *Interviews/entrevistas.* A. Keating (Ed.). New York, NY: Routledge.

Brown, R. N. (2008). *Black girlhood celebration: Toward a hip-hop feminist pedagogy.* New York, NY: Peter Lang.

Brown, R. N. (2013). *Hear our truths: The creative potential of black girlhood.* Urbana, IL: University of Illinois Press.

Brown, R. N., & Kwakye, C. J. (2012). *Wish to live: The hip-hop feminism pedagogy reader.* New York, NY: Peter Lang.

Clay, A. (2012). *The hip-hop generation fights back: Youth, activism, and post–civil rights politics.* New York, NY: NYU Press.

Collins, H. P., & Bilge, S. (2016). *Intersectionality.* Malden, MA: Polity Press.

Delgado, R. (1990). When a story is just a story: Does voice really matter? *Virginia Law Review, 76*(1), 95–111.

Durham, A. (2010). Hip-hop feminist media studies. *International Journal of Africana Studies, 16*(1), 117–135.

Durham, A., Cooper, B., & Morris, S. (2013). The stage that hip-hop feminism built: A new directions essay. *Signs: Journal of Women in Culture and Society, 38*(3), 721–737.

Endsley, C. (2016). *The fifth element: Spoken word as social justice pedagogy.* New York, NY: SUNY Press.

Emdin, C. (2016). *For white folks who teach in the hood . . . and the rest of y'all too: Reality pedagogy and urban education.* Boston, MA: Beacon Press.

Espinosa, L., Chessman, H., & Wayt, L. (2016). Racial climate on campus. Retrieved from https://higheredtoday.org/2016/03/08/racial-climate-on-campus-a-survey-of-college-presidents/

Gaunt, K. (2006). *The games Black girls play: Learning the ropes from double-dutch to hip-hop.* New York, NY: NYU Press.

Gwendolyn, P., Richardson, E., Durham, A., & Raimist, R. (Eds.). (2007). *Home girls, make some noise!: Hip-hop feminism anthology.* New York, NY: Parker Publishing.

Hall, S. (1990). The emergence of cultural studies and the crisis of the humanities. *October, 53* (Summer), 11–23.

Keating, A. (2007). *Teaching transformation.* New York, NY: Palgrave Macmillan.

Lindsey, T. (2016). The #blackfeministfiyah re-up: An introduction. *The Black Scholar, 46*(2), 1–4.

Lindsey, T. (2015). Let me blow your mind: Hip-hop feminist futures in theory and praxis. *Urban Education, 50*(1), 52–77.

Livingston, D. (2016). *Lift off.* Retrieved from http://www.gse.harvard.edu/news/16/05/lift

Love, B. L. (2012). *Hip-hop's li'l sistas speak: Negotiating hip-hop identities and politics in the New Southby.* New York, NY: Peter Lang.

Morgan, J. (1999). *When the chickenheads come home to roost: My life as a hip-hop feminist.* New York, NY: Simon & Schuster.

Parnell, A. (2016, June 29). Affirming racial diversity: Student affairs as change agent. *Higher Education Today.* Retrieved from https://higheredtoday.org/2016/06/29/affirming-racial-diversity-student-affairs-as-a-change-agent/

Pough, G. (2003). *Check it while I wreck it: Black womanhood, hip-hop culture, and the public sphere.* Boston, MA: Northeastern University Press.

Pough, G., Richardson, E., Durham, A., & Raimist, R. (2007). *Home girls make some noise: Hip-hop feminism anthology.* Mira Loma, CA: Parker Publishing.

Rivera, R. (2003). New York Ricans from the hip-hop zone. New York: NY: Palgrave MacMillan.

Sharpley-Whitting, D. (2008*). Pimps up, ho's down: Hip-hops hold on young black women.* New York, NY: NYU Press.

Student Voices

Kevyn Teape

Student, The College of New Jersey

Poet Self-Portrait

My name is Kevyn Teape, and I am a sophomore marketing major and interactive multimedia minor at The College of New Jersey. I am an advocate for social justice as well as a poet/spoken word artist, collage artist, photographer, videographer, creative director, and fledgling music producer.

I was born in the small city of Englewood, New Jersey, in Bergen County. Outside of a short stint of time in Garfield, New Jersey, I lived in Englewood with the rest of my family for a little over the first seven years of my life before moving south to Burlington, New Jersey, where I currently reside.

My freshman year of high school I received praise for some poetry I had written in my spare time. Around this time I started to realize that I enjoyed writing, but it wasn't until my junior year that I started to write poetry on a regular basis. I wanted to write novels and be published as an author. I began writing my first book, titled *Flow*, spring semester in sophomore year of high school and finished it during the summer. After completing the book, I got into a relationship. My girlfriend had gotten me a gift for my 16th birthday in July, and I thought it would be nice to write her a poem back. From there I started writing her poetry every so often until it became a regular activity for me. We broke up first semester of senior year. To that point, I had only written poetry for her, but I decided that I was going to keep writing poetry because I enjoyed it. My friends urged me to perform my poetry and get into spoken word after graduation, but I was reluctant at first. Then one day I tried it out, wrote three spoken word poems, and showed a few friends my work. They were amazed and further encouraged me to showcase my writings. I started my freshman year of college at open mics and events around campus and got to be known around the college community for some of my performances.

Spoken word has had a profound impact on my college experience. It has allowed me in mere minutes to connect with other students on a level that would otherwise have taken considerable time. The feelings and thoughts that I portray when I'm performing are not exclusively mine, and when someone else expresses the same sentiments that you hold, it can create an emotional connection that makes you feel a bond with that person. When this happens, you tend to feel as if the person speaking knows and understands you. I've had people come to me and tell me how perfectly I've described some of the feelings that they have but have struggled to put in words. It's encouraging to hear that your art is relatable and that people enjoy your contributions to the field.

I've been able to develop some friendships with other poets whom I've enjoyed hearing and have shared similar interests in my works. Poetry is what started many of those conversations, but soon after I found many other similarities with those same people outside of poetry. My group of poet friends is diverse, and I've been able to learn more about their unique experiences and the different realities they face because of their different socioeconomic and ethnic backgrounds.

It is a bit difficult to define what I am as a spoken word artist. Whatever I may be, I know for certain that I am the purest representation of my deepest thoughts, ideas, feelings, emotions, and life experiences when I am writing and performing. Poetry is the vocal expression of my life. Through poetry I can express feelings and thoughts I simply don't know how to through any other medium. I can also open up and talk about my own life in implicit ways through use of metaphor and other devices. Poetry is my most reliable outlet when I need to release tension.

When I first started writing, I would write individual poems about a variety of subjects. After a few months or so, my love for writing non-fiction merged with my affinity for poetry, and I began writing conceptual booklets and collections that followed narratives and had clear theses. My most-discussed topics include depression and mental illness, religion, social relationships, death, nature, and social justice. Everything I write about is related to my personal life, as my life experiences directly influence the subject matter.

Social justice and religion are my most discussed topics because they are the most important aspects of my identity. I am an African American male in American society; this part of my identity is an enormous burden as it forces me to be self-conscious. African Americans are discriminated against in society, and many false and inaccurate narratives depict us negatively. I am aware of these narratives and do not want to be judged or treated according to them, so I do everything in my power to avoid them. In my poetry I discuss what I and others deem as "the Black experience" in America, and I also advocate for justice on behalf of Blacks and other minority groups. I am also a feminist and write poetry in favor of the feminist cause.

In addition to being Black, I am also an atheist. My choice to be an atheist has further alienated me at times because there is a lack of support for atheists in the Black community, as we don't make up a substantial portion of the population. I have felt ostracized at times for my religious belief. I write about religion and being an atheist in some of my works in an attempt to normalize atheism and to tell some of my experiences as an atheist.

If I were to use one word to communicate the role that spoken word has played in my life, it would be *liberating*. When I'm writing, I'm free to express whatever I feel moved to write. I can speak on my deepest and darkest thoughts, advocate for social equality, be humorous, and much more. The world is quite figuratively in the palm of my hand, and I always intend to make the most of the power that spoken word gives me.

"Carlos" or "Patrick Swayze"

What do you see when you look at me?
Is there a fire brewing in my eyes
As red as the stripes you hold onto so
Dearly when you claim that you have not profiled me?

What are you listening for when you hear me?
Do you care about what I'm saying
Or does the meter make you forget that it's running until you feel that the price of my bars can't be paid with bills
But my life instead?

What do you feel when you play with my hair follicles?
Does it feel like wool, cotton, sheep,
Or something else more animalistic than humane because
I've noticed you like to pet it as if
It were while you slam my head in the concrete.

What do you taste when my name is across your tongue?
Am I overly salty
Or
bitter over my experiences
Or am I well seasoned to injustice
And seeing that it seems to happen to just us?

I wonder what I am to you everyday when I see you roaming the streets in my neighborhood.
I wonder what you see when you look into the eyes of my brothers because you become so fearful;
I've never seen in them what you do on a regular basis around here.

I wonder what I am to you everyday when I'm playing baseball at the Rec
and I see you parked out on the sidewalk—
And why sometimes you mistake the crack of the bat for a gunshot;
We're only stealing bases but you seem tense as if we were stealing a
diamond.

I can't figure out what I am to you when you claim that you smell
something in the air.
Do you sense something so toxic in the air that you have to strangle all the
oxygen out of me to better ensure my safety?

I guess I'm black like permanent ink:
I can see the impressions I leave when
I'm walking down the street and all eyes are on me.

I know I'm noticeable,
I turn heads like coins
And boy if I had one for every
Five tails pinned on me by the two party system
I wouldn't be broke
And maybe I can be seen as the victim.

To you I might as well be a barren silhouette or a shadow in the alleyway;
A shady individual.
Because you refuse to recognize me for what I am,
You only recognize the color of my skin as if it resembles who I am—
Past
Present
And future if gifted to me.

I ask what I am to you,
And though you've never said it,
I know clearly what your answer is.
Just because I'm Black doesn't mean that I am a villainous character you
have to pay special attention to.
Just because I'm Black doesn't mean that I'm a dirty immoral individual
whose soul needs cleaning.
And one day you'll realize that just because I'm Black,
Doesn't mean I should be treated any differently
Than someone who doesn't share the same skin tone as me.

7

SETTING THE STAGE

Considerations for Creative and Intentional Spoken Word Programming

Anthony R. Keith Jr.

Educational practitioners committed to providing high-quality co-curricular experiences for students must develop a core set of objectives that guide the planning, implementation, and evaluation of their programs, and creativity and intentionality are vital components to the process of developing effective programmatic frameworks. For the purposes of this chapter, I explore spoken word poetry programs as creative vehicles that intentionally foster student engagement and development in educational spaces. Specifically, I highlight themes emerging from a pilot study I conducted on the educational experiences of college-student spoken word artists. I submit that these themes can serve as guidelines for creative spoken word poetry program development.

About the Pilot Study

Schools and community-based organizations that facilitate artistic expression in educational spaces serve as two of the main entry points for youth to engage with spoken word poetry. I was interested in discovering how these students were introduced to spoken word poetry, how they developed as artists, and what role (if any) their educational experiences played in the content of their poems and the style of their performances. I also wanted to know how these students' experiences with spoken word poetry influenced their academic behaviors (e.g., motivation to learn, study skills, and interactions with teachers, administrators, and other students). I conducted a pilot study, for a qualitative methodology class, on the spoken word poetry experiences of three Black male college students. The following key questions guided my novice investigation:

- What does engagement with spoken word poetry in educational settings mean for high school students of color?
- How do high school students of color engage with spoken word poetry during their college matriculation process?

Participants

The first participant, Malachi, was a 19-year-old Black male college sophomore, and alumnus of a college preparatory program I managed for several years. The second participant, Kosi, was a 20-year-old Black male college junior. I met Kosi while serving as a volunteer coach for the DC Youth Poetry Slam Team (DCYST), of which he was a member. My third participant was Eric, a 19-year-old Black male first-year college student. I also met Eric during his time with the DCYST.

I performed one-hour interviews with each participant over the course of one semester, then transcribed and coded the data to discover emergent themes. The questions were organized into three broad categories:

1. *School experiences and academic behaviors*, which focused on study habits, relationships with teachers and other students, favorite subjects, and the school environment;
2. *Spoken word poetry*, which focused on their introduction to the art form, factors that contributed to their growth and development as artists, content of their poems, and their performance style; and
3. *College matriculation*, which focused on the college application process, selecting the best-fit school, choosing a major, and receiving support from families.

The analysis from the pilot study indicates that four key experiences are central to the participant's engagement with spoken word poetry in educational settings:

1. Feeling supported by an affirming school environment
2. Developing confidence through community building
3. Developing a critical consciousness through resisting oppression
4. Connecting poetry to student achievement

Collectively, these four themes can serve as a framework for creative spoken word programming in different types of educational environments. While the focus of my pilot study was on these students' high school experiences, similar outcomes can exist in after-school programs, community-based organizations, and institutions of higher education. I explore each of these themes in the next section as they relate to creative spoken word poetry programming.

Affirming School Environments

Supportive school atmospheres played an important role in shaping the participants' expectations about their intellectual potential and their academic performance. In particular, positive relationships with their teachers and administrators made them feel valued and affirmed. According to Malachi,

> After ninth grade I transferred to a public charter school and it was a little bit better [than his former neighborhood public school]. It was organized. I felt like I had administrative help. I felt like I had a relationship with students and people in positions of power.

Malachi's understanding of power dynamics within educational settings is compelling. He recognized the importance of developing positive rapport with individuals who make decisions that directly affect his school experience. Similarly, Eric shared,

> My teachers loved me, and I loved my teachers. I was on the dean's list most of my semesters. So, my grades were good. Teachers messed with me—just because I was respectful.

Eric's use of the word *love* is indicative of his feelings about a school environment where positive emotional associations between teachers and students are an appropriate motivator for his academic achievement. Furthermore, Kosi established his relationships with his teachers through trust and high expectations. He stated,

> I was always good and always had good relationships with my teachers. They were literally my saving grace. They knew how intelligent I was. They knew what I was capable of. . . . I was always good at establishing relationships with my educators as well as conveying to them that I know the information, and I have a grasp of the information.

Conversely, unsupportive school environments were associated with the students' experiences of meeting minimized expectations. In other words, students' academic performance affected their own expectations of themselves and the expectations of their teachers and fellow classmates. For example, Malachi spoke of this phenomenon extensively when I asked him about his school experiences before transferring to a more affirming school environment:

> When I started off in ninth grade, [the school] was difficult; it was difficult. Not necessarily academically, but just like in terms of the environment and in terms of the administration . . . in terms of providing for the students. I didn't study. I didn't read. I short-ended myself in everything. My grades were great but not perfect; they could have been perfect. That's just always who I was. I was always the smart goofball. I was always that person that, uh, "I got it, y' know," and when I got it, I zoned out.

Similarly, Kosi expressed an awareness of his own intellectual abilities in relation to his classmates, which affected his engagement in the classroom:

> I was never doing the things like I was supposed to at the time, but because I think I was good at catching things. If there's anything I'm good at, it is observing small cues to get on track, or know the answers. Teachers would have the answer on the back of the board, and homies would be like, "Uhhhhhh," and I'd be like, "Bruh, it's on the back of the board! She wrote it right there, fam!" Instead, I'm going to draw comics in class and read books in class because I was bored. . . . I've never been a diligent student in the sense of studying. I've always been self-study to be honest. I always find myself learning fast by myself.

Poetry in Practice

What does this mean for spoken word poetry programming? For a creative program to be effective, the environment must be culturally inclusive and intellectually stimulating. There should be an intentional focus on fostering positive interactions with the poet, the audience, and the program administrators. And while open mic events can invoke a spirit of noncensorship, all participants need to use inclusive language that promotes solidarity. Thus, the host should be mindful of disparaging content and aware of the audience's responses to culturally insensitive performances. Additionally, the environment should feel comfortable and engaging. Placing a microphone in front of a few chairs in a classroom may not garner the same level of participation as hosting an event with music, food, creative décor, and a host who regularly uses call-and-response techniques to keep the audience engaged.

Students should be encouraged either to present poems that focus on specific themes or to collaborate with other artists. I once hosted an open mic poetry event named The Stoop, which reflected not only a cultural space for sharing narratives but also a space that showcased collaborative artistic performances. There were poets performing with other poets, musicians, visual artists, and dancers. Ultimately, we need to consider students as active participants in the collective experience and not simply as passive audience members.

Developing Confidence Through Community Building

Performing poetry publicly can be exhilarating as well as frightening for many people, especially teenage poets. The adolescent period involves a multitude of intellectual, social, and physical developmental changes. The participants in this pilot study expressed developing confidence during this time by learning to love their own voice and being accepted by the poetry community. For Malachi, joining a community of spoken word artists at his school was instrumental in his positive growth and development:

> When I started doing poetry in 10th grade, I got on the stage and was comfortable being vulnerable, and comfortable being assertive, and comfortable being both. [Poetry] really helped me gain a confidence that allowed me to survive, socially. It was really important because I was always the guy that was always worried about what everybody else was thinking about me and was always trying to mold myself into something that was a better aesthetic for everybody else. But when I hit that poetry, I knew that I had a solid community of people that approved of me regardless, right? They were a community of people who didn't ostracize me. . . . It just really helped me carry myself in a way, which was self-satisfying.

Malachi's reference to spoken word poetry as a utility for social survival is a clear indication of students' need for acceptance from their community. His ability to be brave in a vulnerable space speaks volumes to his capacity to develop confidence.

Kosi, however, learned to embrace his voice through spoken word poetry, which granted him confidence in ascribing his identity as a poet. He shared,

> In high school, I went from being quiet and unengaged in class to definitely being a lot more outspoken, and spoken word poetry gave me an opportunity to like my voice. I used to be made fun of in elementary and middle school because I talked funny or because I had a speech impediment. So people would always pick on me, so I wouldn't talk. I would never

say anything. The more and more I got into spoken word, the more people started seeing me as a spoken word artist.

For Kosi, spoken word poetry provided a platform for him to embrace an authentic part of himself that he shielded from others. He became proud of the texture and tone of his voice, which generated a boost in his confidence and self-acceptance.

Eric shared a similar experience when he discovered hip-hop's inextricable connection to spoken word poetry when he joined the DCYST:

> I had a handful of poems that I wrote but I never really performed them. I went to Busboys and Poets on 5th & K for their first youth open mic. I performed one of my raps called the "Ink of the Scholar"—a hip-hop song I wrote a cappella—in a spoken word poet fashion. It's very poetic. The people were like, "Ah!" They went wild! Especially considering the age I was. People came up to me afterwards and were like, "Yo, you were dope, you're the future!" and JT [teacher-poet] who was hosting the open mic told me about the DCYST. . . . Next thing you know, I'm competing at local and national youth poetry competitions as a member of DCYST!

Eric's account of his first time performing spoken word poetry in an out-of-school setting illuminates the significance of community programs that focus on empowering youth through creative artistic expression.

Poetry in Practice

Creative spoken word poetry programs are not just opportunities to entertain and engage students. They also serve as pathways for students to achieve self-actualization. Thus, it is critical that the audience and the host understand the importance of celebrating every poet's performance, whether at an open mic or a poetry slam competition. At a traditional open mic event, individuals sign up on a list to present their poems for the audience in a noncompetitive environment. At a poetry slam, however, poets receive scores from impartial judges and are required to keep their performances within a specific period of time or format. Institutions opting to host a creative spoken word poetry program should be mindful of the difference; I have attended numerous events presented as poetry slams when they are in fact open mics. In either case, the audience must always clap for the poet and for the poem. A positive reception from the audience can boost poets' confidence and assure them that they are in the presence of a supportive community. Furthermore, institutions can foster the growth and development of poets who regularly attend open mic events by helping them form a club or a team that writes and performs together, which helps sharpen their performance skills through peer feedback.

Developing a Critical Consciousness Through Resisting Oppression

Spoken word poetry continues to serve as a tool for social action, creative agency, and equality. Poets are able to proliferate the voices of the oppressed in an accessible medium that not only sparks a critical consciousness but also increases the public's awareness of injustice. The participants in the pilot study discussed their experiences with social inequities, which served as the foundation for their involvement with spoken word poetry and the content of some of their poems. For example, Eric expressed his understanding of oppression and resilience through his discovery of "truth":

> Truth . . . starts on a very personal basis and a social political basis as well. Like, Malcolm X and everything . . . I started to understand how systems of oppression work, starting with my own—the system of oppression that I'm up under as a young Black man . . . as a Black person in general . . . racism, White supremacy, and how that has impacted the world and shaped the world that we now have, and just understanding the history behind it and the science behind it as well. When it comes to White supremacy, it's a social structure. It is a social structure, but where did the social structure come from?

He continued,

> I was in music class one day in fifth grade, and we were learning "The Star-Spangled Banner," and I ended up going home early right after that class . . . and when I got home, I was laying in the bed just thinking to myself about the last line that's like "land of the free and home of the brave" [and I added], "so said the Whites, but the African slaves . . . ," and thought, *Oooooo I should become a rapper!*

Eric's early attempt to comprehend the lyrics to "The Star-Spangled Banner" correlates with his search for the truth about social structures that perpetuate racial inequity. He used creative artistic expression to contextualize his understanding of the history of racism and White supremacy.

Relatedly, Malachi shared how his racial experiences shaped much of the content of his poetry:

Generally, [poetry topics] are about a social issue that aligns with my identity. I talk about Black things. I talk about Black things. I talk about Black
things. Most importantly, I talk about Black things. A lot of it has been
realizing how complex Blackness is, and how complex Blackness is, and
how complex the systems against Blackness are. As I've gone through my
journey, it's really been a different step. So, at each stage of my life, I've
written poems wherever I am in my Blackness. The social issue that reflects
where I am. Now I'm trying to write about the concept of surviving—the
concept of surviving, not just life or death, but the parts of ourselves that
we kill off. Like, emotion is something that Black men are taught to just
kill off. Sympathy, empathy—things that we're just taught to throw away.

Like Eddie, Malachi reflected on a similar experience with understanding systemic oppression at an early age:

I think that it is interesting, particularly as a kid—no, particularly as a
Black child—a lot of times we're often told that a lot of the positive qualities about ourselves are wrong, ya know? And that some of the qualities
that we have that are perceived as negative aren't actually negative, ya know?
And so I think it was interesting being an intelligent Black kid in DC
public schools, particularly like elementary school, I was always questioning what I was doing wrong. Ya know?

These students' capacities to recognize structural racism and articulate their rejection of oppressive ideologies are indicators of their development of a critical consciousness. Poetry and rap became platforms that
catapulted their use of artistic expression to share cultural narratives about
social justice.

Kosi also reflected on his experiences with social inequities as a youth:

[Race] mattered in elementary school and middle school because Cheverly
[a suburb of Washington, DC] is an interesting space because you do have
the old tobacco families. White families [are] still there, but you also have
[Black] migration from DC to that area as well, so it was always kind of
like a small concentration of Black wealth. My parents were middle-class
and educators. People around us were doctors and lawyers like that.
Cheverly has a different economic background, so I'd be in spaces in which
case my assumed economic status was always lower than it necessarily was.
But my mom, being from the Bronx, she let me know that we were always
broke [laugh], but this place is where all of the Black wealthy families threw
their kids to be honest. It was replete with this Black upper middle class,
and this was the first time I was like, "Wow, yo! Your parents own three
McDonald's! They don't work at the McDonald's?" [laughs] But it was

funny because all of the educators were White women and all the students were Black kids. . . . It was just this weird phenomenon.

When I asked Kosi how those experiences informed the development of his poems, he shared,

> I think a lot of what I try to do with my spoken word now is go back to my past, and what I've been doing recently is foraging my past for when spoken word poetry and slam poetry had its effect on my work. . . . I do see that they created a canon or like an aesthetic that is good its own right. . . . I think a lot of what I was trying to do was prove at the high school age that I was good enough to be in the same conversation as these [White] people.

Poetry in Practice

Students' exposure to issues of poverty, racism, sexism, and homophobia occurs every day. Schools, however, considered as great equalizers, rarely provide opportunities for students to engage with these issues inside the classroom. Most students articulate their feelings and ideas via social media posts and engage in a digital dialogue moderated by the number of likes, comments, and emojis on their pages. However, creative spoken word poetry programs—especially open mic events—serve as nonpunitive, cathartic spaces for students to express their frustrations about social injustice and to share their personal experiences with oppression. Educational organizations that value youth voice can benefit from listening to how students are feeling about their world. Student-poets should be able to openly critique policies and inspire others to take action. In my professional career I have witnessed students share more opinions about school leadership and administration at an open mic poetry event than I have at school town hall meetings. Students have the intellectual capacity to develop and express a critical consciousness; spoken word poetry can serve as a vehicle to foster awareness of oppression and promote social justice through the arts.

Connecting Poetry to Student Achievement

The final theme suggests that achievement for student spoken word artists is a process that aligns students' artistic endeavors and their authentic identities. All three participants in this pilot study incorporated their personal narratives in their college application process. Malachi's passion for social justice and poetic activism influenced his school choice and development of his personal college essay. He wrote a creative statement about his life as a Black male youth growing up in an underresourced urban community:

Poetry really helped me get into these schools. When I started using poetry—particularly as social justice and activism and speech against inequality—that helped my narrative become a little more fluid . . . a little more centered. I write poetry, I perform poetry, and I have a book. I go to protests all of the time. I came from this, and this fuels my poetry, which also fuels my activism, which is also why I want to go to an Ivy League institution. What really helped me get into school was having a narrative that was . . . real. Expressing that narrative through poetry helped me polish it up for the essay. It seemed like one product, and I knew what I was doing. I did it on purpose, and I don't feel bad about that.

Malachi's authentic narrative served as his impetus for applying to highly selective institutions that lacked racial and ethnic diversity. He was confident that most schools would admit him based on merit alone, but he wanted to be on a college campus where he could express activism through poetry. Malachi is a first-generation college student who received acceptance to numerous colleges and universities, including three Ivy League institutions. When I asked him how his family felt about his success, he shared,

Just because their resume doesn't match it, doesn't mean that their product is not as good, if not better. I think that's what really helped me—knowing that people can have so much to offer but can be reduced to so little, such as a GPA or a transcript. I have to see bigger than that. It's not my job to discriminate against people with this elitist mentality where it's like education is the only out . . . like it is the only predictor of how much somebody has to offer.

Malachi received his college acceptances with humility, which he knew could have been mistaken for pretentiousness. Poetry invoked a spirit of confidence in Malachi and a desire to resist oppression, which ultimately led to his success.

Kosi was also confident, but instead he wrote about his involvement with spoken word poetry as a part of his college essay:

I remember everything I was doing at that moment was to look good enough. . . . I think my GPA was a 3.6 in high school, so I knew I could get into college, but . . . I was gonna have to be particularly shiny or interesting. Thankfully, those leadership positions and spoken word helped. . . . I was literally always Student Council president because the day of [the election], I freestyled a speech. [Laughs] A boy with an Afro freestyling speeches! Yeah, yo! But spoken word is something that I wrote about [in my college applications] . . . about my relationship with performance and stuff like that. When I think about my time with the DCYST, and think [all of the] hours of performance time over the course of a few years, I look back and think, *Wow, my stage time!* When you think about the time on stage, [it's] immense. I think about how comfortable I am hosting open mic events now, how comfortable I am not knowing what poem I am going to do, but still be able to carry on something anyway. It is because I've been doing show after show, after show, after show.

Kosi's consistent engagement with spoken word poetry is indicative of his capacity to commit to an endeavor and be persistent. He not only developed confidence and an arsenal of poems to share but also understood the inextricable relationship between performance and achievement.

Eric took an approach similar to Malachi's and transformed a poem about his life into one of his college essays:

I have a [poem] called "Who Am I?" where I tell my story more or less. . . . I kind of just did that in essay form, kind of to be real . . . and, with the added factor of what is it, why is it that you're trying to come to college, what are your goals, and what do you want to study? It was just my story with all of that added in there. . . . It made it a whole lot easier because I didn't have to do a whole lot of thinking about it necessarily. I just kind of transferred the format. I switched up the way in which it was expressed to a degree. Instead of making sure all of it rhymed and flowed . . . I mean it still flowed, but in its own way . . . in an essay way. Essays I can take a stance on something and speak truth. That's what it comes back to. In whatever format I can speak truth and spread truth. I love it, you know? Like, if I had to write an essay about some shit I don't care about, I'm not even gonna write that essay.

Eric's account suggests that spoken word poetry is an artistic expression of truth that has utility in academic spaces.

All three participants are currently enrolled college students and are actively involved in the spoken word poetry community on and off campus. In a follow-up chat with Eric, he shared,

I've been doing a lot of performing on the university side of things because most of these people do not know me, have not heard my material, so I'm able to perform as if it's something new. It's new to them, so I felt more comfortable doing that. I actually just hosted an open mic this past Thursday that went really well. It was real dope. It was in the common area, with about 40 people. It was very intimate and dope. Everybody that came up and did their thing was real dope, too. But there was a competition they had that helped me get a lot of exposure on campus, too, because they had three aspects of the competition. You had hottest emcee, hottest

DJ, hottest beat maker or producer. I was going for emcee and I won that joint! . . . People heard me do my song "Sunshine" and they were like, "Yo, you're dope!" and that actually helped me gain a lot of exposure on campus. I mean people actually come up to me pretty often, like, "Hey!" and it's wild because I was doing goal setting before the year started and one of my yearly goals for this year was to be recognized as the best emcee on campus and off campus. So, I kind of got that in campus lockdown!

Spoken word poetry truly helped Eric gain confidence in vulnerable spaces. As a first-year student in college, Eric secured his status as a spoken word artist on campus and accomplished a goal.

When I asked Kosi about his academic interest and career path, he shared,

I'm an individual studies major here! [laughs] I went from being an engineer to being computer science to being into film to being in studio art, and thought, *What the hell am I doing?* My parents were like, "What the hell are you doing?" All I want to do is write about weird things, right? My writing so far has expanded beyond spoken word, and I'm enjoying a lot of written poetry and short stories and science fiction. I made this major called Transmedia Storytelling, and it looks at how we can disperse narratives through multiple media platforms and media channels while each media channel contributes something new about the narrative. It is more so like a media consumption paradigm. I'd like to be like the Black Walt Disney. I realize through science and film and all these things I was building that I'm very invested in creating worlds and writing about them, and exploring them, but I definitely acknowledge my leadership potential because of all of the work I've been doing and all the people who empowered me to create these spaces, look to me to complete the spaces. So I definitely see myself being a writer, story editor, and moving on up to being able to produce a live piece of work.

Clearly, there is an extricable link between spoken word poetry and student achievement.

Poetry in Practice

A student's motivation to learn how to write poetry and perform poems for an audience could be an indicator of the student's self-efficacy and academic motivation. Thus, any creative spoken word poetry program must have academic utility. Academic departments and student affairs offices can play a key role in developing these types of cocurricular learning opportunities. I taught a course at a university that offered students an elective credit to spend the semester with me learning about spoken word poetry and inclusive language, which was a collaborative effort to foster diversity on campus among the Office of Residence Life, the Office of Multicultural Affairs, and the College of Education. I also judged a poetry slam competition between teachers and students at a local high school; the students won, of course, but spoken word poetry minimized the power dynamics that often exist in educational spaces. Thus, any school or community-based organization interested in developing a creative spoken word program must consider the potential for academic utility or student goal setting.

Conclusion

The students in my pilot study expressed their involvement with spoken word poetry as a beneficial resource and a creative outlet for their survival and success. The students demonstrated that spoken word poetry programs are creative vehicles that intentionally foster student engagement and development in educational spaces. Collectively, these students' narratives suggest that creative spoken word poetry programming should

- strive for inclusion and affirmation,
- help students develop confidence through community building,
- guide students in developing a critical consciousness and resisting oppression, and
- connect poetry to student achievement.

The following additional implications could be of interest to urban school districts, youth development organizations, arts-based educational programs, English/language academic departments, and postsecondary institutions:

- Education leaders can instigate partnerships with community-based organizations that offer performance arts opportunities for youth as a part of school programming and spoken word poetry as supplemental material for developing students' written and verbal communication skills.
- Educational researchers can expand their scope of exploring the relationship between the performance arts and student achievement to be inclusive of spoken word poetry.
- Policymakers and civic leaders can consider allocating resources to schools and communities that are experiencing a rise in student achievement as a byproduct of spoken word poetry programming.

8

SCALING UP FOR SUSTAINABILITY

Hip-Hop and Spoken Word as Vehicles for
Transnational Inclusion

Marla L. Jaksch

Hip-hop and spoken word have served and continue to serve as important vehicles for personal and collective political identity, community building, transformation, inclusivity, and social change—as the previous chapters clearly testify. Among the many significant contributions that hip-hop theory, education, and culture have made to social justice praxes have been the insistence on creating spaces—for challenging inequalities and social norms as well as redefining norms and spaces. These challenges center on the development of tools and approaches forged out of an abundance of historic and contemporary resilience and resistance strategies and doing so *without* an abundance of financial or institutional support or space. Alternative pathways toward sustainability are important to trace and acknowledge.

Each chapter in this book has foregrounded the possibilities of hip-hop and spoken word for institutional spaces and for our students—whether students are "bringing wreck" or are transformed by their encounters with hip-hop praxis (Pough, 2003). In this chapter I explore how we might extend the possibilities of hip-hop and spoken word into untapped networks, locations, and relationships that move us through the past and present and into the future. In order to consider how we do this work, I bring together hip-hop feminist studies with the concept of Afrofuturism(s). I do so in order to provide a theoretical framework and set of creative practices that expand available notions of collaboration and leadership that are useful in creating a lasting, meaningful inclusivity. I follow this overview with an articulation

117

of a critical praxis of resistance and healing. I conclude the chapter by sharing some examples of the types of theorizations I describe, as well as hint at some of the continued barriers in achieving the goals of this work and how we might address those challenges.

Hip-Hop Feminist Studies and Afrofuturism(s)

Hip-hop is, and has always been, a transnational phenomenon—drawing specific links to Africa and the diaspora through beats, words, movements, ideas, dress, culture, politics, history, and action. As time has gone on, hip-hop has extended beyond specific physical, virtual, and geographic locations and boundaries. In fact, and for some time now, it is hard to travel anywhere in the world where an aspect of hip-hop culture is not widely known, heard, seen, or practiced. However, hip-hop feminist studies focuses on what has been overlooked and has remained marginalized, unnamed, and acknowledged—specifically, women's and girls' contributions to and engagement with hip-hop as a political project. Zenzele Isoke argues,

> Hip-hop feminism effectively challenges and transforms power structures, social order, and widespread cultural practices, and is proving to be an efficacious intersectional strategy for understanding the complex identities and difference in Women's Studies and across academic disciplines. Simultaneously, hip-hop feminism engages effective grassroots community-based social justice movements across *transnational frameworks*. (In Durham, 2010, 134n1, emphasis added)

The types of community-based social justice movements that Isoke refers to address topics that connect communities across time and space, such as efforts focused on quality education as a human right, as well as attention to the specific barriers for women and girls in receiving an education. Girls from New York to Tanzania share some of the same barriers to education in regard to violence and sexual harassment, as well as to science, technology, engineering, and mathematics (STEM) topics (Crenshaw, 2015; Devlin, 2017; Peter & Malyi, 2013; Smith, Happauch, & Van Deven, 2011); Williams, Phillips, & Hall, 2014). Therefore, adopting theoretical approaches that have the capacity to account for the specific types of marginalization that girls of color face while simultaneously accounting for their differences is a necessity in building inclusive social justice–oriented programs and strategies to move us forward.

Like intersectionality and hip-hop culture, *Afrofuturism* existed in practice long before a term was developed to describe it. Mark Dery (1993) first coined the term in his article "Black to the Future." There he begins to develop a language to describe engagements with Black speculative fiction that addresses themes and concerns of African Americans in relation to "20th-century technoculture—and, more generally, African American signification that appropriates images of technology and a prosthetically enhanced future" (Dery, 1994, p. 180).

For Alondra Nelson (2002), Afrofuturism is really a way of looking at the world—an epistemology that centralizes Black life, resilience, and resistance along with an articulation of alternative aspirations and speculation about the future, combined with connections to technologies and technoculture. Afrofuturism is also described as a "philosophical, technocultural vernacular perspective" rooted in "heterodox form[s] of cultural production originating in socio-spatial temporal practices of black urban dwellers in North America" after World War II (Anderson & Jones, 2015, pp. 127–128). This way of thinking, which has been most deeply rooted in Black arts movements of science fiction and jazz, has transformed into a highly intersectional, trans-disciplinary, and transnational way of thinking that includes "metaphysics, ethics, digital hermeneutics, geopolitics and several other dimensions of humanities and sciences" (Anderson & Jones, 2015, p. 128). Due to the ways that Afrofuturism alters and reworks accepted approaches or belief systems in an attempt to create something that more adequately captures past, present, and future events, ideas, and possibilities, it seems to offer a lot of potential for higher education generally—and student affairs and social justice education more specifically. It offers a particularly interesting way of thinking about sustainability, which is a critical issue when discussing creating transformative educational experiences.

What's Epistemology Got to Do With It? Building Alternative Standpoints

Key to both hip-hop feminist studies and Afrofuturism is an investment in alternative stories about who we are and who we can be, specifically for girls and women of color. Hip-hop is a significant tool for knowledge production, but the knowledge produced is often not legitimized (Jenkins, 2011). Critical epistemological approaches critique universalist, dualistic, and essentialist knowledge projects by making visible bias in the mechanisms, legitimating forces, and institutions that produce subjects and their "other." Feminist epistemological projects are concerned with how intersectional identity categories influence our conceptions of knowledge, practices of inquiry, and justification—from a feminist standpoint. Such projects are also about how knowledge is produced and by whom.

The right to self-definition is a key function of Black feminist thought, a standpoint emerging from the Combahee River Collective but further developed by Patricia Hill Collins (1990). Collins (1990) argues that the power to name one's own reality, especially as it may contradict what she calls *controlling images* by producing and making visible alternative understandings that reject the dominant group's definition, is a core function of freedom from oppression.

Recent work in hip-hop feminist studies centralizes the importance of epistemologies that emerge from girls' everyday lived experiences. Durham, Cooper, and Morris (2013) argue that the utility of hip-hop feminism comes in large part due to the "continued investment on being in but not of the academy" (p. 723). One way this happens is through research, pedagogy, and community-based projects that concern themselves with democratizing forms of knowledge that facilitate better understanding of how subjectivity is produced, performed, represented and policed in the United States and beyond (Love, 2012).

Readers may wonder what an Afrofuturist, hip-hop feminist–informed project in the academy might look like. In the next section, I share an example of an ambitious project that models cross-institutional, collaborative, peer-to-peer, transnational community-engaged learning.

Girls Do STEAM!

In the spring of 2015, Girls Do STEAM! was launched in Trenton, New Jersey, with a full-day workshop and build-in. The acronym STEAM represents the inclusion of art and design into science, technology, engineering, and math to give participants exposure to hands-on learning that challenges them to think critically and creatively and lets them apply important content knowledge in meaningful ways. Hosted in a building leased by The College of New Jersey (TCNJ) in downtown Trenton—Trenton Works—the workshop brought 10 high school girls together with 2 TCNJ women's and gender studies majors (and STEM lovers) and 3 facilitators with the purpose of building 2 standalone solar "suitcases" that would provide light to an all-girls school on Pemba Island in Tanzania. These suitcases are compact, portable, solar-powered units that provide easy, efficient lighting and electricity. The organization We Share Solar provided the materials for the solar suitcases.

The development of the program emerged from a series of conversations in which we, a small group of feminist artists/activists/teachers, expressed with each other our shared interests in and frustrations with feminist girls' "empowerment" programs, especially those at the intersections of art and technology. Some key areas of our frustration centered on lack of the following:

- programs that applied a critical race or intersectional framework in their girls' programming, especially in relation to STE(A)M;
- critical application of the arts in youth programming;
- youth programming that emphasized peer-to-peer learning;
- opportunities for students to engage one another across time and space that was not Internet-based; and
- ways to promote this work in which the girls could speak truth to power to those with the power and resources (in a nongimmicky, nonexploitative way).

For example, we noticed a trend with girls and STEM programming that remains largely skills-based, with little to no attention to intersections of race, class, gender, ability, and sexuality. Colleges and universities want to recruit girls, especially girls of color, but remain committed to practices, materials, and pedagogical approaches that have been deeply criticized, particularly by feminists in the field (Williams, Phillips, & Hall, 2015).

Despite residing in different cities, working at different institutions, and possessing different areas of expertise, we realized that collaborating and pooling our collective resources would be the best way for us to address concretely some of the barriers to serving our communities and our students. From these conversations, Girls Do STEAM! was born. In addition to the workshop and build-in with 10 girls selected from Both Hands Artlet (with full curriculum), our collaborator, Both Hands Artlet, was established by Bentrice Jusu from her personal experience and belief in the arts to transform lives of teens in Trenton, New Jersey. It serves as a stable center and source of art, mentorship, and positivity for teens in Trenton. The organization embraces and caters to all teens, regardless of their personal backgrounds ("delinquents" to high-achieving scholars) or experience with art (from no experience to advanced). Because we believe that everyone bears an art, we ironically dismantle the traditional definition and associations of *art* as an objective, aesthetic realm and allow all teens to discover their own abilities, use the available tools of expression and learn from their peers and mentors, and discover their hidden or unexpressed potential. Beyond the age and residential restrictions, the only set of requirements for participation includes the willingness to fully engage in the program and to keep an open and positive attitude. The emphasis for this program is on personal growth, exploration, self-expression, fun, and creativity. Ultimately we expect that participation in these activities will not only benefit students in the short run but also open up multiple avenues through which students will pursue their education and futures, through high school and beyond (see www.bothhandsartlet.org).

We also established a peer-to-peer installation training session with 4 TCNJ students and a solar installation service-learning program with 10 John Jay College of Criminal Justice students at an all-girls STEM school with 20 girls on Pemba Island. We concluded with an invitation to the International Day of the Girl (IDG) presentation at the United Nations in New York.

The goals of the Girls Do STEAM! Trenton workshop were to use the building of stand-alone solar suitcases (see We Share Solar, wesharesolar.org)— for girls in another area of the world challenged by energy insecurity—as a vehicle for building community, raising self-perceptions, demystifying STEM, creating a space to explore intersectional identities related to STEM, and understanding why people are energy insecure.

We broke the workshop into the following parts:

- introduction with poetry/spoken word;
- exploration of concepts (energy insecurity, tech justice, feminism, colonialism, intersectionality, racism, sexism, etc.);
- introduction to the suitcase and reflection;
- lunch with a presentation about where solar would be installed;
- finish build;
- photography; and
- critical self-reflection through spoken word—cipher.

We began the workshop by explaining the objectives of the day and significance of STE(A)M through the building of a solar suitcase. Each section of the workshop was facilitated by a different person or small group, with the actual building being led completely by two TCNJ students.

The Girls Do STEAM! workshop consisted of girls ages 16 to 20 from Trenton high schools who had an interest in STEM and art. Several of the girls were enrolled in STEM programs in their schools but noted that, due to a lack of support, their engagement with STEM was largely theoretical. Many of the girls came from homes that were consistently energy insecure, with one of the participants describing the strategies that her family took, particularly in the winter, to keep on the heat or electricity.

One of the organizers shared her own story about the safety and health hazards she encountered growing up in her family trying to keep on the lights and heat. Sharing our experiences in this way further informed the project, for while the solar suitcases would not be installed in our homes, it gave the whole process purpose. What produces energy insecurity and for whom? How does this insecurity affect girls and women in Trenton and Tanzania? Imagine the joy when, at the end of a long day of assembly, the girls flipped the switch and the lights came on!

The workshop successfully produced four solar units that were installed at an all-girls STEM school on the island of Pemba. The entire United Republic of Tanzania is just 14% electrified. Pemba receives its only electricity through a 20-megawatt submarine cable from mainland Tanzania. Energy insecurity, coupled with gender norms and inequalities, deeply affect education for women and girls. And, like in Trenton, energy insecurity produces dependence upon candles, oil (kerosene and other impure oils), or (diesel) generators that tend to be dirty as well as health and fire hazards that serve only as stopgap measures to long-term needs. Therefore, the second workshop focused on how to collaboratively install and teach our partners how to use and maintain the system so that reliance upon nonrenewable energy sources would not continue to burden the school or the girls, who were largely studying by candlelight—a major expense for school-age youth.

An additional workshop, held at an artists' collective in Trenton, brought together students who had already installed these solar suitcases in the same region to teach the group of 10 John Jay students how to install, problem-solve, and teach the system to others. Further, several members of the group built junction boxes, light cords, and switches. Very little of this workshop was facilitated by the organizers; rather, the workshop modeled hands-on, peer-to-peer teaching. Collective and collaborative, the workshop aimed to ready the students who would be traveling and installing the system to be prepared and supported, providing an opportunity to discuss the ways that energy insecurity is a part of hip-hop feminist education. Hosting the workshop in an art collective warehouse, where working artists forged their creative seeds into tangible ideas, was a purposeful choice to inspire but also make concrete the links between STEM and the arts: STEAM. STEAM approaches art as a technology and creativity as a necessary site of problem-solving.

This group successfully installed the solar units and facilitated a workshop and cipher. In each of the workshops, we introduced poetry, spoken word, and journaling as important methods of critical self-reflection and community building. Participants were encouraged to write, perform, and document throughout their experiences.

Those words (in statements, poetry fragments, and letters) and actions made their way across the world and back again to find their home in the halls of the United Nations. On October 11, 2015, the girls from Trenton were invited to attend the IDG Speak Out, and a short documentary film featured the girls building the solar units, reflecting in their own words and capturing them in their home community. Girls are disproportionally impacted by uneven development (in the United States, Tanzania, and around the globe), a problem compounded by racism, classism, and misogynoir. Girls are the least likely to be listened to and to have their ideas respected. Hearing the girls from Trenton link their own energy insecurity to those in Pemba made visible what's at stake when we systematically keep girls and women from being a part of the solution.

In her 2015 track "One Woman," we hear Akua Naru rap about her lived experience as a Black woman—in all of its rich, beautiful, complex, and painful fullness. At around 3:26 in the recording, we hear the voice of Tricia Rose, hip-hop feminist scholar, discuss the power of the cipher—those with the mic, especially amplified mics. Rose's voice is layered over jazzy soul beats, scratches, and beat breaks that are simultaneously slow, discordant, frenetic, and full of energy. Rose asks us to consider what happens to the spirit of community and power that exists around the mic, getting to speak and having your words be amplified, if Black women's voices are muted or are not welcome—especially when those voices move out of the accepted and expected scripts of sex and relationships and instead pivot to questions of power or discussions of trauma and violence. Further, Rose wonders about how those among the less heard become a part of the metaphorical cipher. She maps the journey that women and girls in hip-hop have made when they take the mic, demand to be heard, and compel us to listen.

GDS presents an alternative approach for doing social justice education. As a program that is transdisciplinary—and that foregrounds collaboration among faculty, student affairs, students, and community partners from different colleges in the United States and abroad—GDS highlights different pathways toward inclusivity as praxis. For inclusivity to become a part of the practice and culture of student affairs, hip-hop– and spoken word–inflected approaches need to be adopted. This program gives a very complicated view of what a hip-hop, feminist, inclusive, and activist-oriented service-learning program might look like. It includes deep and intentional education, peer-to-peer instruction, and international collaboration, and it uses spoken word and hip-hop pedagogies as forms of reflection and processing. A program of this nature is also an example of what a powerful partnership across the campus might look like. In this case, a women's center, cultural center, service-learning department, women's studies department, and Africana studies department might all come together to create a complex and impactful learning experience.

As Afrofuturist visual artist Wangechi Mutu (Lynch, 2010) notes, women and girls are "barometers," and due to their marginalized status, they are intimately vulnerable to the fluctuation of social and cultural norms. When we listen to what women and girls have to say about their lived experiences, we learn not only about them but also about the ways that various systems, structures, and institutions affect them. Girls and women do not lack a voice or perspective regarding the barriers in their way; rather girls and women lack a platform and entry into places and spaces that matter and that allow their words and ideas to be heard, amplified, and legitimated. It is the practice of not seeing, hearing, or legitimating voices and perspective that leads to transformation and social change.

Study Abroad as Hip-Hop Social Justice Praxis

For more than 10 years, I have designed, organized, assisted with, and implemented study abroad programs across Africa, although I have spent most of my career working in East Africa and Tanzania in particular. My introduction to this work came through a relationship with a former Black Panther couple who live in exile from the United States in the Arusha area of Tanzania. Since 1991 the United African Alliance Community Center (UAACC) has acted as a community development center serving the youth of the local rural community on the slopes of Mount Meru. UAACC also welcomes and hosts individuals and organizations, as well as colleges and universities, in exchange for supporting and teaching in their ongoing youth programming. UAACC works to connect youth from the United States to youth in East Africa, largely through the arts and social justice work.

Beginning in 2006 I developed and led an arts- and social justice–focused program for the UAACC. In the following years, the program extended to additional arts, social justice, and leadership programs, visiting many community program locations across mainland Tanzania and the islands of Zanzibar. The first trip began and ended with a cipher—a combination of participants, in many different languages, styles, and approaches but with a similar goal—to uplift the voices of youth and bring them into dialogue.

Almost every program I have created has been a joint faculty and student affairs endeavor and has aimed to reimagine what a typical study abroad program could be and do. My foremost goal was to develop programs that allowed students to travel outside of a European context. I also focused on devising programs that traveled for shorter periods of time due to financial constraints and other obligations that many of my working-class or poor students confronted. Further, program itineraries were created with students' interests in mind. For example, I created an intake form that provided me with details about interests beyond a student's major, especially their musical, arts, and social justice–related interests. I would invite international artists, activists, and young people with shared interests to community dinners so that students could network and enjoy each other's company—not just interacting with "experts" in the field.

We also don't meet solely in academic spaces. Rather, most learning happens in the community or in community spaces. Being intentional about what is being shared, where, and by whom is a way to bring a critical hip-hop consciousness to the development of a study abroad or community-engaged learning program. As with marginalized communities in the United States, meeting with youth in global spaces can be very powerful, as they tend to have unique vantage points about what is happening in their community and country. Students often have brilliant and untapped ideas about solving social problems (Collins & Bilge, 2016). Additionally, spending time with my students outside of our shared, fixed spaces allowed for new and different types of relationships to emerge.

Many colleagues ask how such programs are possible—specifically, how do we pay for them? That's a legitimate question, given the cost of many programs and the limited resources of our students and the institutions in which we serve. But precisely because of this economic precariousness we have sought alternative solutions. In part, partnerships between academic and student affairs faculty and staff open up new ways of thinking through this old problem, as well as access to different resources. Moreover, there are ways to pay for study abroad beyond student loans. One of my goals has been to learn about funding opportunities and become knowledgeable about what constitutes a competitive application, which requires putting together a fellowship-advising timeline, identifying those within the institution who can support the development of a strong application, providing letters of support, and mentoring the students through the process. It also means being honest with students in regard to how the process works and doing as much as you can to demystify it. Too many of my students come to me initially eager to travel but overwhelmed at the prospect of applying for competitive funding to support their travel, once they realize what the process entails, or even where to begin.

The organization Brioxy (brioxy.com), established in 2015, is the embodiment of the power of opening up new pathways. Founder B. Cole, as a first-generation college student, recognized that success is determined by more than smarts and hard work and entailed navigating invisible rules that shape how one gets ahead—including what scholarships to apply for and how. She understood that she lacked the social capital—the interpersonal connections that connect someone to key information and opportunities—that most of her privileged peers enjoyed. Cole states,

There are all of these hidden rules around the way that you were supposed to show up in our culture, and many of us have no clue how they even operate. It doesn't matter if I just give you the opportunity to apply for a scholarship—if you don't know how to compete for it, you don't know how to ask for the right advice, you're not going to be successful regardless of your talent. And that's the same around job interviews, buying a house, taking out business loans, and so on. So I had made it my life's work to do this coaching individually, but I'm only one person, and I wanted a way to scale it up. I wanted to build a peer network and a platform for sharing information that would provide young people of color with a kind of insider guide to the world. (PolicyLink, 2016)

Study-abroad programming has historically functioned in this way, too. Who gets to travel and where is connected not only to interest and resources but also with support in navigating the system. The goal of Brioxy is revealed in the following:

Linking thousands of young people of color together to change the opportunity landscape in this country. We are on the cusp of the largest demographic shift this country has seen in almost 500 years. Today, 70% of those under 25 in California are young people of color. But by 2040 it will be the nation. We created Brioxy to organize ourselves, invest in each other's dreams and advance health, education and economic policy that will improve all of our lives. By becoming a member of Brioxy you have a stake in our collective future. (Brioxy, 2017)

Brioxy has an available list of resources and fellowships, and through membership one can get additional support and services. Student affairs staff might consider joining through institutional membership. Despite the odds and the forces telling us that we cannot establish programs that rethink inclusivity through hip-hop social justice frameworks, we continue to dream and create networks within our institutions that can support this work.

The Socio-Spatial and Temporal Practices of Hip-Hop Resistance and Resilience

But when, even in the imaginary future—a space where the mind can stretch beyond the Milky Way, to envision routine space travel, cuddly space animals, talking apes and time machines—people cannot fathom a person of non-European descent a hundred years into the future, a cosmic foot has to be put down. (Womack, 2013, p. 7)

When we think about *sustainability*, we think about something lasting, at a certain rate or level, and with the structures and frameworks to support it. In the context of higher education, the term also takes on additional meaning—such as making something permanent, which includes the resources, especially financial, needed to build and maintain it. Within higher education we also describe this process as the *institutionalization* of a program, value, or tradition. Certainly there are reasons for fighting against, or at least having a critical positioning in relation to, such a notion of sustainability. In the final section of this chapter I consider ways to rethink sustainability though an Afrofuturist, hip-hop feminist praxis—to encourage us to imagine a praxis that moves us closer to social justice and the inclusive community of our dreams. What does this space look like? Where is community likely to occur?

Transnational inclusion need not take place outside of the United States or even off campus. It can be cultivated through investments in the stories our institutions are willing to tell and share and by acknowledging embedded cultural knowledge that institutions share in hidden and overt ways. Sociologists often describe *social capital* as shared cultural knowledge. Cultural theorist Pierre Bourdieu (1986) describes *social capital* as cultural knowledge that is shared among people based on their similar background and experiences. This capital is exchanged and shared in the space in which it is produced or in another space in order to build one's capital. Social capital can work in exclusionary ways through a particular kind of closed circuit. Part of what colleges replicate are places of belonging a priori; in other words, this network and social capital are produced and exchanged through traditions that are not open to all. Colleges' identities tend to be fixed and become the very thing that makes them resistant to social and other types of change, therefore serving as a challenging but necessary site for this work. As Cole explains, her goal in establishing Brioxy is for the collective organization to serve as a

> catalyst for changing the opportunity infrastructure within communities of color and to ensure that youth of color are driving growth within their own communities. The rising generation is more diverse than ever before. Youth of color will be the ones shepherding the economy in the coming decades, and you have this cohort of incredibly talented young people in this country who are standing ready to lead, to develop, to build all kinds of things. And we're not going to wait for someone else to give us what we need. We're going to organize ourselves. We have to all link up in order to make that happen for each of us.

A student of mine shared that hip-hop music served as a site of connection, space making, and community building:

As a child growing up I often felt that I lived in two very different worlds. I was born and raised within the inner city of Newark, New Jersey, to *Bur-kinabé*, West African parents who immigrated to the United States. Within my childhood I never knew where I belonged or felt I had a good understanding of my personal identity. I was a Black girl in "White" America and a first-generation West African in the "Black" inner city. As a result of my reality I never thought I fit into any spaces I occupied. In other words, I was too African for the Black kids and too American to be considered African. This often resulted in my deep internal and external struggle growing up in regard to figuring out who I was and how I defined myself. Growing up within a time where I was struggling with my identity was extremely difficult for me. Because music is very therapeutic and often has meaningful messages and themes, I often turned to music to help relax me in regard to my inner and outer battles.

Social spaces operate both as a product and producer of change in the environment. The built environment of the university is intrinsically meaningful; it has stories to tell us about culture, policy, economics, security, and so on. Hip-hop feminist studies and Afrofuturisms highlight the dialectical connections between space and social relations by suggesting that we not only occupy space but also are produced by it. That Afrofuturism and hip-hop provide recognition of space as produced rather than given indicates that social relations are both producing space and shaped by it. Although Lefebvre (1974) first wrote about the use of space in colonizing everyday life, the work of hip-hop and Afrofuturism has been to decolonize space and the right to produce uncolonized space.

Student affairs staff are uniquely positioned to create or facilitate the creation of spaces for students to create new traditions. As another student of mine noted,

A huge part of my identity is rooted in music and in the music that I listen to. Growing up in an environment that stifled the open expression of emotions made it incredibly difficult for me to express myself, especially as someone who is very sensitive and feels everything so intensely. This silencing—compounded by my traditional Chinese upbringing, where I was told to not speak up about my opinions, to not "rock the boat," and to just "take it" and not retaliate when I was wronged—made it extremely confusing and challenging to understand myself and the turbulent storm that was everything that I was feeling. The emotions and feelings that I could not put into words and articulate, I found the words and language to describe [them] through listening to hip-hop music. Hip-hop gave me a way to explore and understand my pain. Hip-hop taught me introspection and how to engage in self-reflection.

In an attempt to get feedback, feel the reciprocal power of spoken word, and process poems of a complex nature, one of my students began setting up informal "listening parties"—outside, in free outdoor spaces that do not require student organization affiliation or the navigation of a complicated university room reservation system, which can take days or weeks to receive confirmation. The goal was to facilitate a more creative and flexible approach that emphasizes word of mouth and other social media strategies to bring together an audience. The advantage of this approach is that it allows poets to perform more informally, to engage in a dialogue about the work, and to converse about the issues the poems inspire. I appreciate this approach because it decenters faculty and student affairs staff and recenters student voices, creativity, and community building. Creating a sustainable program might look like building a program that becomes entrenched in the campus culture for more than 17 years, like Toby S. Jenkins created at the University of Maryland, or it might involve creating a culture of agency among students on your campus. A lasting culture of student agency passes on a legacy that informs and directs current and future students to know that they are free to create and develop whatever inclusive, open, and authentic space they desire on the campus. In this way, it becomes much less about sustaining any one particular program and more importantly about sustaining a campus culture that privileges student voice.

References

Anderson, R., & Jones, C. E. (2015). *Afrofuturisms 2.0: The rise of astro-Blackness.* Lanham, MD: Lexington Books.

Bourdieu, Pierre. (1986). The forms of capital. In Richardson, J. G. (Ed.), *Handbook of theory and research for the sociology of education* (pp. 241–258. New York, NY: Greenwood.

Brioxy. (2017). Our story. Retrieved from www.brioxy.com/about

Collins, P. H. (1990). *Black feminist thought: Knowledge, consciousness, and the politics of empowerment.* New York, NY: Routledge.

Collins, P. H., & Bilge, S. (2016). *Intersectionality.* Malden, MA: Polity Press.

Crenshaw, K. (2015). Black girls matter: Pushed out, overpoliced, and underprotected. African American Policy Forum. Retrieved from https://static1.squarespace.com/static/53f20d90e4b0b80451158d8c/t/54d2d22ae4 b00c506cffe978/1423102506084/BlackGirlsMatter_Report.pdf

Dery, M. (1994). Black to the future: Interviews with Samuel R. Delany, Greg Tate, and Tricia Rose. In *Flame wars: The discourse of cyberculture* (pp. 179–222). Durham, NC: Duke University Press.

Devlin, H. (2017). AI programs exhibit racial and gender biases. Retrieved from https://www.theguardian.com/technology/2017/apr/13/ai-programs-exhibit-racist-and-sexist-biases-research-reveals

Durham, A. (2010). Hip-hop feminist media studies. *International Journal of Africana Studies, 16*(1).

Durham, A., Cooper, B., & Morris, S. (2013). The stage hip-hop feminism built: A new directions essay. *Signs, 38*(3), 721–737.

Jenkins, T. (2011). A beautiful mind: Black male intellectual identity and hip-hop culture. *Journal of Black Studies, 42*(8), 1231–1251.

Lefebvre, H. (1974). *The production of space.* Oxford, UK: Blackwell Publishers.

Love, B. (2012). *Hip-hop's li'l sistas speak: Negotiating hip-hop identities and politics in the new south.* New York, NY: Peter Lang.

Lynch, W. (2010). On view: Wangechi Mutu's "One hundred lavish months of bushwhack." *Inside/Out* [web log]. Retrieved from https://www.moma.org/explore/inside_out/2010/03/18/on-view-wangechi-mutus-one-hundred-lavish-months-of-bushwhack/

Naru, A. (2015). One woman. On *The Miners Canary.* Cologne, GermanyL The Urban Era.

Nelson, A. (2002). Introduction: Future text. *Social Text, 20*(2), 1–15.

PolicyLink. (2016, June 17). Changing the opportunity landscape by networking youth of color: An interview with Brioxy founder B. Cole. Retrieved from http://www.policylink.org/blog/brioxy

Pough, G. (2003). *Check it while I wreck it: Black womanhood, hip-hop culture, and the public sphere.* Boston, MA: Northeastern University Press.

Smith, J., Happauch, M., and Van Deven, M. (2011). *Hey Shorty! A guide to combatting sexual harassment and violence in schools and in the streets.* New York, NY: Feminist Press.

Williams, J., Phillips, K., and Hall, E. (2015). Double jeopardy? Gender Bias Against Women of Color in Science report. Retrieved from http://www.uchastings.edu/news/articles/2015/01/double-jeopardy-report.pdf

Womack, Y. (2013). *Afrofuturism: The world of Black sci-fi and fantasy culture.* Chicago, IL: Chicago Review Press.

EPILOGUE

Toby S. Jenkins

I originally wrote this poem for my colleague and coauthor of this book Crystal Leigh Endsley as she departed her job in the cultural center at Penn State University. I share it here as a poem dedicated to the staff members who bring spoken word to campus and the brave students who grab the mic and bare their souls.

Riding Into the Sun

Your voice jumpstarts vehicles of change
It sparks creativity
It channels energy
It cranks up young souls
It recharges batteries that are old
It turns over lives
It transforms a used and abused
Ride
Into a shiny new
Baby blue
Show car in our eyes
And you are behind the driver's seat as the guide
And we're proud to admit
That we all admire your whip
And we're just happy that we got to sit shotgun for a bit . . .

Your spirit awakens minds
It quietly creeps up from behind
And unlocks doors and opens blinds
And because of the work that you do
Because of the excellence you exude
Because of the foot that you put
into the life work that you stew
We say thank you

ABOUT THE EDITORS

Toby S. Jenkins, PhD, is an assistant professor of curriculum studies at the University of South Carolina (USC). Prior to USC, she served as a faculty member at Georgia Southern University, the University of Hawai'i Manoa, and George Mason University. Her professional background includes 10 years of experience as a student affairs administrator at The Pennsylvania State University and the University of Maryland. Her first book, *My Culture, My Color, My Self: Heritage, Resilience, and Community in the Lives of Young Adults* (Temple University Press, 2013) was named to the American Association of Publisher's List of the Top 100 Books for Understanding Race in America. Her research interests focus on how communities of color use culture as a politic of social survival, a tool of social change, and a medium for transformative education. She is also interested in the ways in which culture influences students' perceptions of the purpose of education and their commitment to community-based leadership.

Crystal Leigh Endsley, PhD, is assistant professor of Africana studies at John Jay College of Criminal Justice, City University of New York. Her first book, *The Fifth Element: Social Justice Pedagogy Through Spoken Word Poetry* (SUNY Press, 2016) explores spoken word poetry as a tool for social justice, critical feminist pedagogy, and new ways of teaching and learning. Endsley is an internationally renowned spoken word artist. Recognized by *Cosmopolitan Magazine* as a "Fun, Fearless Female," Endsley is both performer and professor, and she works to serve her community as an artist, activist, and academic. Her most recent scholarship-activism focuses on how spoken word poetry and performance can connect girls, impact their communities, and inform government policy. She directed the creative performance of spoken word at the United Nations for International Day of the Girl in October 2016. Her TEDx talk is available at www.youtube.com/watch?v=_k2j22g-fIY8 or get in touch @drcrystalleigh.

Marla L. Jaksch, PhD, is an associate professor of women's, gender, and sexuality studies with affiliate appointments in the African American Studies Department and the International Studies Program's Africa concentration at The College of New Jersey. She also serves as the founding coordinator of competitive postgraduate fellowships. She attended The Pennsylvania State University where she received a dual-title PhD in women's and gender studies and art education. Her research interests include neocolonialism, development, and digital cultures; science and technology studies in sub-Saharan Africa; transnational feminisms; and expressive, material, and digital culture. For more than a decade she has developed and facilitated arts and social justice focused community engaged learning programs and community based-research—locally and globally—from Trenton, New Jersey, to East Africa.

Anthony R. Keith Jr. (Tony) identifies as a poet, an educator, and a nerd. As a poet, Keith has traveled around the world teaching through poetry and empowering young people to engage in the art of spoken word. He volunteers as coach for Washington DC's Youth Poetry Slam Team and most recently featured at Washington National Cathedral's Martin Luther King Jr. celebration. As an educator, he strives to ensure social justice and equity is at the crux of his curriculum, pedagogy, and professional practice. He currently serves as director of programs for Love of Children, an educational services provider operating outside school time for marginalized youth in Washington DC. As a nerd, Keith is a perpetual student; he holds a BA in communication from the University of Maryland College Park, an MEd in college student affairs from The Pennsylvania State University, and is a PhD student in education leadership at George Mason University.

With the increased accessibility of cameras, the ability to engage in image production has become widely available. Individuals, including college students, faculty, and administrators, narrate the social world in new ways using visuals. In promoting visual literacy, this book offers new opportunities for student development administrators and faculty to utilize the visual sensory modality and image-based artifacts to promote student success and belonging which are critical outcomes of higher education.

Sty/us

22883 Quicksilver Drive
Sterling, VA 20166-2102   Subscribe to our e-mail alerts: www.Styluspub.com

Also available from Stylus

Critical Mentoring
A Practical Guide
Torie Weiston-Serdan

Foreword by Bernadette Sánchez

"This is a brilliant book. It is also an extremely useful one. Torie Weiston-Serdan has accomplished the great achievement of writing something that is immediately accessible, deeply thoughtful and theoretically engaged, and of practical use to all those engaged in youth mentoring. It is also beautifully written. *Critical Mentoring* has the potential to change the paradigms of practice in the field."
—*Viv Ellis, School of Education, Communication and Society, King's College London*

At this juncture when the demographics of our schools and colleges are rapidly changing, critical mentoring provides mentors with a new and essential transformational practice that challenges deficit-based notions of protégés; questions their forced adaptation to dominant ideology; counters the marginalization and minoritization of young people of color; and endows them with voice, power, and choice to achieve in society while validating their culture and values.

This book offers strategies that are immediately applicable and will create a process that is participatory, emancipatory, and transformative.

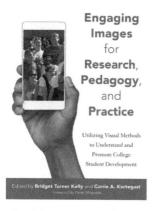

Engaging Images for Research, Pedagogy, and Practice
Utilizing Visuals to Understand and Promote College Student Development
Edited by Bridget Turner Kelly and Carrie A. Kortegast

Foreword by Peter Magolda

This book introduces practitioners and researchers of student affairs to the use of images as a means to gaining new insights in researching and promoting student learning and development, and understanding the campus environment. Visual research methods can surface and represent ideas in compelling ways and augment the traditional written word and numerical data methodologies of social science research. The purpose of this book is to provide informative, rich examples of the use of visuals to understand and promote college student development research, pedagogy, and practice.

(Continued on preceding page)